SPECIAL MOMENTS

In African-American History: 1955-1996
The Photographs Of

MONETA SLEET, Jr.

EBONY Magazine's Pulitzer Prize Winner

SPECIAL MOMENTS

In African-American History: 1955-1996
The Photographs Of

MONETA SLEET, JR.

EBONY Magazine's Pulitzer Prize Winner

Compiled and edited by Doris E. Saunders
with Introduction by Gordon Parks Sr.
and Afterword by Lerone Bennett Jr.

JOHNSON PUBLISHING COMPANY, INC. Chicago, New York, Los Angeles, Washington, London, Paris, Johannesburg, S.A.

Copyright by Johnson Publishing Co., Inc.
First limited edition, 1998
Library of Congress Cataloging in Publication Data (CIP)
Sleet, Moneta Jr., 1926-1996
Special Moments In African-American History: 1955-1996, The Photographs of Moneta Sleet, Jr.
EBONY Magazine's Pulitzer Prize Winner

Compiled and edited by Doris E. Saunders,
with Introduction by Gordon Parks
and Afterword by Lerone Bennett Jr.
Includes index

ISBN O- 87485-087-8

Book Design by: Raymond A. Thomas

Distributed by St. Martin's Press

Printed in the United States of America

dedication

This book is dedicated to the memory of Moneta Sleet, Jr.,
Staff Photographer for Johnson Publishing Company, Inc. 1955-1996,
and
as he dedicated his exhibitions to his wife, Juanita, to his children,
Gregory, Michael and Lisa, to his grandchildren, Moneta, III, Ashlee and Kelsi,
and to the memory of his parents, Ozetta and Moneta Sleet, Sr.

"You try to develop the sensitivity and the **'eye'** to see that very *special moment."*

Moneta Sleet, Jr.

INTRODUCTION

portrait of a friend

UPON meeting or leaving Moneta Sleet the air was always thick with his gracious smile. His demeanor, akin to a lock without a key, allowed one to enter his presence without a moment of difficulty.

I have come to want two things from other human beings. One is honesty. The other is courage. Moneta was endowed with both. So it is understandable that those who grew to respect him did so without concern for the lack of either virtue. He gave strength to my belief that truly fine journalists tend to be fine human beings. Wed to the needs of common people, he made a profession of being earthbound–avoiding the shadowy traits of those who wish others ill.

Regretfully, Moneta died much too young. But just how long was he supposed to live, fifty years or a hundred? The important thing is that he moved among us with love and without any signs of perversity. Now, we who knew him can raise our glasses and toast those good years that we did share with him. And those years cannot be taken out of time. Nothing could stop the flow of his spirit–not even the huge silence that replaces his presence.

This fine collection of his work will help keep that spirit flowing. We could ask no more than the justice of its existence. It carries us to silken places, bristling places and the markets of misery we suffer. It shows us what we were and what we are. Finally, it warns us that returning to the past is to return to imprisonment.

Photographers come and go. The works of the good ones stay on and on, ripening with the years. The cameras of some tell us that all is well. While those of others shout that everything's bad. Moneta, having lived through all the shadows of everydayness, embraced all conditions, mixed them generously with compassion and presented them to our curious eyes. He spoke for those who died for worthy causes, for those born yesterday and for those who will be born tomorrow.

And we never grow weary of what he had to say. There are certain photographers who grow so big they fail to fit in ordinary doorways. Overtaken with self-esteem, they forget that they are considerably less important than their subject matter. Not Moneta. He was a student of modesty, constantly aware that his subject was capable of teaching him, of helping him to take another look upward. A glance backward tells me that his sensitivity, so lacking in some of his compatriots, kept him on the right track. That sensitivity, spawned during the depths of his childhood, never deserted him. It was still burning like a bonfire when he was summoned into the long rivering night. Undoubtedly death had the right to choose his time of departure. But this, Moneta's volume of existing work, will cling to its right for a much longer life. That's the way things are.

GORDON PARKS
New York, N.Y.
August 29, 1997

CONTENTS

INTRODUCTION
**Portrait of a Friend
by Gordon Parks Sr.** **VII**

PART ONE
FAMILY ALBUM **3**

PART TWO
THE PHOTOGRAPHS, 1955-1996 **15**

The Civil Rights Movement **16**

Africa and The World **51**

Politics, Social and Public Figures **88**

Celebrations and Inaugurals **111**

Family, Food and Fashion **127**

Entertainment, Sports and the Arts **141**

PART THREE
FAMILY ALBUM COMPLETED **163**

Death and Funeral of Moneta Sleet, Jr. **172**

AFTERWORD
Lerone Bennett Jr. **175**

Acknowledgements **177**

Index **179**

part one:
FAMILY ALBUM

beginnings

OZETTA ALLENSWORTH SLEET

MONETA SLEET, SR.

O N my father's side, my great-great-grand-
mother was a full-blooded Choctaw. My father
was a teacher and the business manager in a vocational
school in Paducah, some 80 miles away. He was home
only on weekends.

M Y mother's people went back to Germany or Holland. My
mother had been a teacher and she read to us a lot. My
mother did the day-to-day bringing up, and she was a very fine lady.

G ROWING up in Owensboro, Kentucky, where I was
born, February 14, 1926, was a real pleasant experience.

MONETA SLEET, JR.

MONETA, JR., AGE 3

EMMY LOU, AGE 3, AND MONETA, JR., AGE 6

O WENSBORO was at that time a segregated town; I guess the population was about twenty-four to thirty thousand people. In most instances like this, the Black community is closely knit, so we knew everybody. Although I couldn't go to the school right across the street from me, I had to pass that school and go way down to the segregated elementary and high school. This may sound like a contradiction, but despite the segregated pattern, my school years were a good, wholesome experience for me.

I think then the teachers took more interest in you than today. They were interested in your total personality. They knew your parents. They knew your place in the community. In spite of being segregated, the teacher tried to get out of you all that was possible. We learned a lot. I knew I was somebody. I never thought I was less than anybody else.

W HEN I ask myself what makes me tick, what motivates me or what makes me take the type of photographs that I take, it is basically my family, and the family tradition from which I come. A strong father and mother who encouraged me to do what I wanted to do, who said, 'This is what you want? Just go ahead and try it.'

MONETA SLEET, SR. in his office at Vocational School, Paducah, Ky.

I must have been maybe nine or ten years old when my parents gave me a box camera, and I just started fooling around and taking pictures of the family. I was too young then to think in terms of it as any sort of career thing. I went on to Western High School, and the Chemistry teacher, Mr. Ernest Thurston, had a little camera club. He started a few of us out in it. And we would go off into the makeshift darkroom in a little bathroom and develop pictures. And I became fascinated by it.

FAMILY PHOTO: MOTHER, FATHER, EMMY LOU AND MONETA, JR.

E DUCATION *was certainly stressed in our early years. With both of our parents being teachers, we just understood there wasn't any question about whether you were going to college. It was just understood that you went through the whole procedure; we understood that you did the whole bit; elementary school, the high school and on to college. When it was time for me to go to college, my father's mother took me aside. She told me to go up there and study hard and do well. 'Don't disgrace the family name!' she said. She was a little lady, about 5' 1", but she was a very strong woman. You paid attention to what she said. Which I did. I went to Kentucky State College.*

KENTUCKY STATE–ALPHA PHI ALPHA MEN (SLEET C., R., REAR)

W E *weren't rich by any means, but we weren't poor. At least, we certainly didn't think of ourselves as being poor. I went on to Kentucky State where the dean of the school, then Dr. John T. Williams, was quite an accomplished photographer. In fact, we had a real professional-type studio on the campus. Dr. Williams was a friend of my father, and my father had asked him to look after me. He gave me a job working as his assistant, along with his chief assistant, George Stewart, who was graduating. I kind of fell into it. I observed and had a chance to work with him every day. Psychology was his field, and he was a master at handling people. I learned a great deal from Dr. Williams, especially how to deal with people and portraiture. We would shoot all the kids on the campus; we would cover all the sporting events that took place. I worked my way through school, working in his studio and also working in the office cleaning up.*

MONETA SLEET, JR., U.S. Army World War II, served in the CBI (China, Burma, India) Theatre of Operations.

THEN, in 1944 during World War II, I went into the army. In one sense, segregation as a negative part of my life reached me rather late. I think the first big sign of it was on the army troop train. We were going to Fort Lewis in Washington. We stopped in Butte, Montana, for a rest stop. I went into a bar to get water. I picked up the feeling of being unwelcome. At the same moment, I saw a sign on the wall. It said, 'We reserve the right to refuse service to anyone.' None of us could get anything to drink. We were all Black. It hurt me even more, for I had always thought the Northwest was surely the promised land. I talk about it very little. But it is there. I hated it, but I kept it all inside. I served in India and Burma with the 93rd Engineers, an all-Black unit. That time in India has always stayed with me and always will. When we got there, we stayed for a short while in Calcutta. Our camp was not yet ready in the interior. It was very hot. The American base had a pool. So did the British army base near us. We soon learned that the American pool was open only certain days to Black soldiers. But we were welcome any day at the British pool. We were not fighting troops. We could not be at the time. For the most part, Blacks were in some sort of supply work. But we were in the army. We were fighting for our country. And we were segregated. The British owed us nothing. Yet they welcomed us any time.

8

I was a staff sergeant when I came out of the service in 1946. I had pretty much decided I wanted to go into photography and study under the G.I. Bill. My father had ideas of my going into the diplomatic corps and a lot of other things like that. My Dad said, 'Well, what are you going to do to make money?' So I said, 'What I'll do is go ahead and get my degree,' since I had three years toward it anyway. I was a business major; I figured getting that degree would serve me in good stead. Then, after that, I could go ahead and pursue photography. So I finished up the one year, earned the business degree and then went on to New York for a six-month course at the School of Modern Photography and enrolled at NYU in the School of Journalism.

JUANITA HARRIS, a 1948 Hampton Institute graduate and a young high school teacher in Princess Anne, Md.

MONETA SLEET, JR., photographer

MEANWHILE, Dr. Williams moved to Maryland State College at Princess Anne, where he invited me to come and set up a Department of Photography, which I did. I worked there as an instructor from 1948-49 and then decided that I wasn't quite ready to settle down to teaching. I wanted to pursue the more active end of photography.

THE time there wasn't wasted. I met Juanita Harris, a young schoolteacher in Princess Anne. Neet, as I called her, was the woman who was to be my wife.

I completed the master's degree in Journalism at New York University, thinking at that time of both writing and photography, the real photo-journalist type. I found out pretty rapidly that that is difficult to do. I tend to be a perfectionist, and I have to concentrate on one thing at a time.

WHEN I graduated, I spent a few months as a sports writer for The Amsterdam News, a weekly paper in New York City. After working at it awhile, I came to the conclusion that I was probably a better photographer than a writer. Writing was very hard for me...So I made the decision to angle for the photography end. When Our World had an opening in the photography department, I decided to go there since I could not find a job both writing and taking photos.

HARLEM HOSPITAL EMERGENCY ROOM, 1951

I took the job at Our World, where one of my first professional assignments was in the emergency room at Harlem Hospital, New York City. It was very revealing. It is a very rude cultural shock to watch what happens on Saturday night when people come in with all sorts of bruises and cuts and what have you. Watching this young intern work was a fascinating experience and a rewarding one from the photographic point of view as well.

LITTLE GIRL in Superior, W. Va., 1953

ON another story for Our World I had to go into West Virginia to do something on a family that lived in the coal fields and document what life was like for them. I roamed around and made some contacts with various groups. I talked to the Urban League people and NAACP and located a family that was willing to take me in and let me photograph their life for a short period of time. One day, I saw this pretty little girl with the torn dress, and I took her picture.

*M*EANWHILE, *Neet and I had become parents of our first child, a son, Gregory.*

ON PHOTO ASSIGNMENT for *Our World*, Sleet is in Rio de Janeiro, Brazil, 1954

*W*HEN Our World *magazine folded in 1955, I was offered a job at Johnson Publishing Company's* EBONY *magazine. I took it. I have been there ever since.*

part two:
THE PHOTOGRAPHS,
1955-1996

"DURING THE CIVIL RIGHTS MOVEMENT, I was a participant just like everybody else. I just happened to be there with my camera, and I felt and firmly believe that my mission was to photograph and show the side of it that was the right side."

Moneta Sleet, Jr.

the Civil Rights Movement

MRS. ROSA PARKS sparked the Montgomery Bus Boycott when she defied segregation rules on public transportation in Montgomery, Ala. She refused to give her seat on the bus to a White passenger in 1954. This photo in 1956 has Rev. Martin L. King, Jr. at left.

A YOUTHFUL DR. MARTIN LUTHER KING, Jr., leader of the Montgomery bus boycott, with wife, Coretta, and infant Yolanda on steps of the Dexter Avenue Baptist Church, Montgomery, Ala., 1956.

DR. KING TALKS WITH MAN whose head was hurt during bus boycott, Montgomery, 1956.

DR. AND MRS. KING push Yolanda in stroller, 1956.

AT THE APOLLO THEATRE, Mrs. Gertrude Ward, mother of Clara Ward, and Rev. Thurman Ruth, gospel disc jockey, took time out to pray for the success of the Montgomery bus boycotters.

BACKSTAGE AT THE APOLLO THEATRE, Clara Ward of the Ward Singers leads a prayer service while her mother, Mrs. Gertrude Ward, Apollo employee Russell Cooper and Ward Singer Katherine Parham, eyes closed, join in prayer.

National Deliverance Day of Prayer, led by Adam Clayton Powell, Jr., March 28, 1956

REV. ADAM CLAYTON POWELL, JR. (top, r.) prays as the Day of Prayer is opened and is shown as he addresses the group at the Manhattan Center. Rev. Dan M. Potter (top, l.), executive secretary of the Protestant Council of New York, confers with Rev. Adam Clayton Powell, Jr. and Rev. E. D. Nixon, who represented the bus boycotters in Montgomery, Ala. Rev. Nixon, Montgomery, Ala., Pullman porter and treasurer of the Montgomery Improvement Association, came to New York to represent the 50,000 bus boycotters. Crowd scene of praying people (bottom, l.) at Manhattan Center.

IN AN APRIL 1962 raid on a Muslim Mosque in Los Angeles, Ronald T. Stokes, an unarmed Black man, was killed by police. In a 1963 New York City rally, Malcolm X carries a poster blow-up of Stokes.

T HE *autopsy stitches were plainly displayed on his (Stokes) bare upper torso. At that time, Malcolm was not often welcomed on the platforms of many of the rallies. He was considered by some circles to be rather radical. But Malcolm always had his way of getting attention. So he was at the back of the rally...just standing there quietly, not saying a word, just holding up this photograph that had been displayed in the Los Angeles newspaper.*

March on Washington, 1963

ON AUGUST 28, 1963, more than 250,000 people of all races and creeds took part in the March on Washington. A. Philip Randolph, the Brotherhood of Sleeping Car Porters founder and AFL/CIO vice president, had been promising the march for over twenty years. In 1941, when he threatened such a march, President Franklin D. Roosevelt, under the prodding of Mrs. Eleanor Roosevelt and Dr. Mary M. Bethune, produced Executive Order 8803, creating the Fair Employment Practices Commission. Under Randolph's leadership, it was determined by a coalition of civil rights groups, churches and other organizations that it was time to demonstrate the ongoing need for jobs and freedom.

SAID A. PHILIP RANDOLPH in his remarks to the assemblage, "The March on Washington is not the climax to our struggle, but a new beginning, not only for the Negro but for all Americans, for personal freedoms and a better life. Look for the enemies of Medicare, of higher minimum wages, of Social Security, of federal aid to education, and there you will find the enemy of the Negro; the coalition of Dixiecrats and reactionary Republicans who seek to dominate the Congress...We, here today, are only the first wave. When we leave, it will be to carry the civil rights revolution home with us, into every nook and cranny of the land. And we shall return, again and again, to Washington in ever-growing numbers until total freedom is ours."

AMONG THOSE IN THE FRONT LINE leading off the march were (l. to r.) John Lewis, chairman of the Student Nonviolent Coordinating Committee (SNCC); Matthew Ahmann, executive director, National Catholic Conference for Interracial Justice; The Congress of Racial Equality (CORE) National Chairman Floyd McKissack; Rev. Martin Luther King, Jr. of the Southern Christian Leadership (SCLC); Rev. Orange; Rabbi Joachim Prinz, president of the American Jewish Congress; Rev. Eugene Carson Blake of the National Council of Churches; National Urban League head Whitney Young, Jr.; Roy Wilkins, executive secretary, NAACP; March Director, A. Philip Randolph, Brotherhood of Sleeping Car Porters and AFL/CIO vice president; and UAW-CIO President Walter Reuther. Ted Brown (dark suit and badge) of the Leadership Conference on Africa and advisor to A. Philip Randolph is right front.

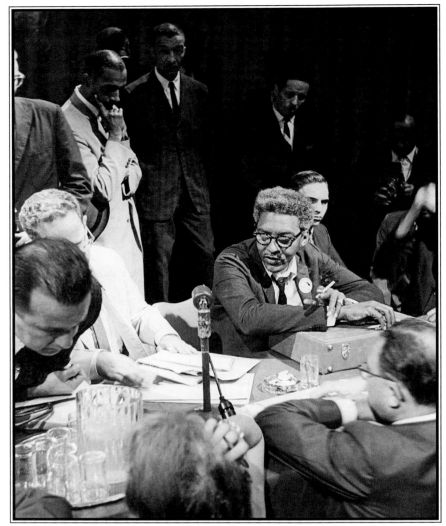

BRILLIANT TACTICIAN BAYARD RUSTIN, as assistant director to Randolph, was in charge of logistics, strategy and management of the massive crowd of celebrities, politicians and ordinary folk, from tots to senior citizens, disabled veterans and athletes. They all came.

SAMMY DAVIS, JR. and Roy Wilkins speak with reporter.

THEY SAID:

NOW is the time to rise from the dark and desolate valley of segregation to the sunlit path of racial justice...There will be neither peace nor tranquility in America until the Negro is granted his citizenship rights...No, we are not satisfied and we will not be satisfied until justice rolls down like water and righteousness like a mighty stream...

MARTIN L. KING, JR.

IT is simply incomprehensible to us here today and to millions of others far from this spot that the United States government, which can regulate the contents of a pill, apparently is powerless to prevent the physical abuse of citizens within its own borders...We expect the passage of an effective civil rights bill.

ROY WILKINS

WE must support the strong, we must give courage to the timid, we must remind the indifferent and warn the opposed. Civil rights, which are God-given and constitutionally guaranteed, are not negotiable in 1963.

WHITNEY M. YOUNG, JR.

WE are involved in a serious social revolution. But by and large American politics is dominated by politicians who build their career on immoral compromising and ally themselves with open forums of political, economic and social exploitation...If we do not get meaningful legislation from the Congress, the time will come when we will not confine our marching to Washington, D.C. We will march through the South, through the streets of Jackson, through the streets of Danville, through the streets of Cambridge, through the streets of Birmingham.

JOHN LEWIS

JOSEPHINE BAKER flew in from Paris for March.

MARIAN ANDERSON SANG *He's Got the Whole World in His Hands* and Mahalia Jackson (above) brought them to their feet singing the spiritual *I've Been 'Buked and I've Been Scorned.*

AMONG THE MULTITUDES participating were Undersecretary Ralph Bunche, The Rev. Fred J. Shuttlesworth of Birmingham, NAACP director Mrs. Daisy Bates, Joseph Rauh, vice president for civil rights of the Americans for Democratic Action, Clarence Mitchell, director of the Washington Bureau of the NAACP, Arnold Aronson, secretary of the Leadership Conference on Civil Rights, Josh White, Lena Horne and comedian Dick Gregory.

JACKIE ROBINSON AND SON , DAVID

HARRY BELAFONTE with group at March

Mississippi Freedom Summer–1964

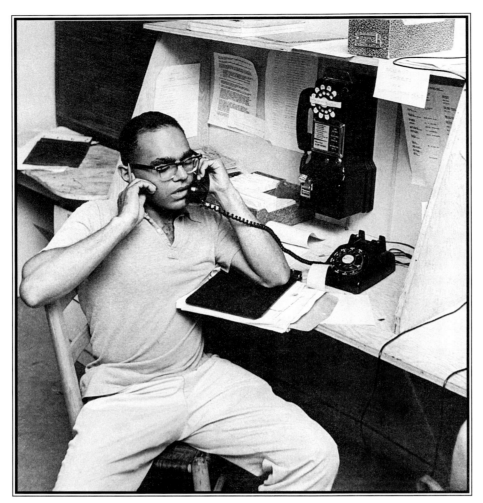

A COALITION OF SNCC, CORE, THE NAACP AND SCLC launched a two-month crusade across the state of Mississippi with the blessing of the National Council of Churches. Under the direction of Robert P. Moses, field director for SNCC, it was called the Mississippi Freedom Summer 1964 Project. Over 700 volunteer students, teachers, social workers, ministers and lawyers worked to increase voter registration, raise levels of academic achievement among African-American high school students, reduce illiteracy and increase skills in arts and crafts. Further, they worked to promote a slate of Democrats to challenge the seating of all White Democrats at the 1964 Democratic Convention. COFO Director Bob Moses (l.) gets report of Holly Springs beatings on phone from Jackson (Miss.) headquarters. Moses, a Harvard University graduate, devoted full time to the volunteer movement.

VOLUNTEERS RESEARCH FEDERAL PROGRAMS in order to be able to acquaint local Blacks with Social Security, federally subsidized housing, job retraining, farm subsidies and educational opportunities. Their discussions centered on the best method for distributing this information with follow-through to the communities where the need was great.

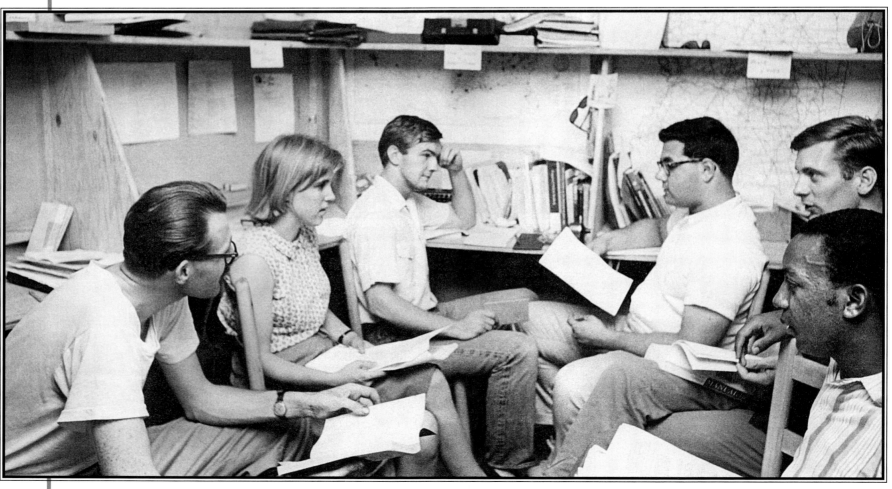

HAVING INVITED U.S. REPRESENTATIVES to Mississippi to see firsthand what conditions were really like, veteran COFO worker Stokely Carmichael gives background briefing on the Mississippi situation in COFO's Greenwood (Miss.) office to U.S. Congressmen Phillip Burton (D-Calif.) (seated, back to camera), Augustus F. Hawkins (D-Calif.), William F. Ryan (D-N.Y.) and SNCC's John Lewis. On his return to New York, Rep. Ryan charged that "general collusion" existed between "White vigilante groups, and some local police." He indicated there was "no reason to believe that it did not extend to the disappearance of these boys (Michael Schwerner, Andrew Goodman and James Cheyney)." The bodies of the three young volunteers were recovered August 4, 1964, and twenty-one men were arrested on December 19 and charged with violating their civil rights by "apprehending, assaulting, shooting and killing them."

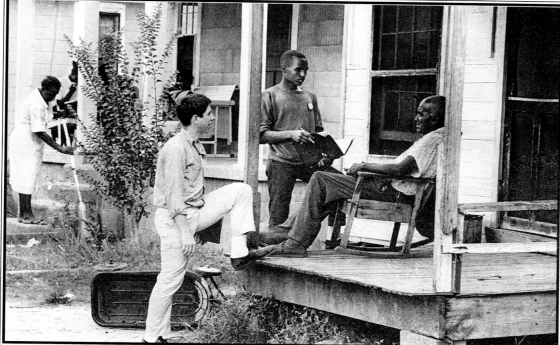

VOLUNTEERS CIRCULATE in communities throughout the state to explain the process of registering to vote to the residents who must overcome decades of indoctrination against participation in the process.

ANN POPKIN, RADCLIFFE COLLEGE STUDENT from Long Island, N.Y., teaches simple dance steps to children during a recess outdoors. Building in the background is the COFO Community Center in Vicksburg, which offered youngsters arts, crafts and a variety of recreational activities.

What Manner Of Man

A BIOGRAPHY OF
MARTIN LUTHER KING, Jr.
BY LERONE BENNETT, Jr.

WHAT MANNER OF MAN –The announcement of the awarding of the Nobel prize was made in September 1964. Mr. John H. Johnson determined that there would be a major biography of King available for the ceremonies in Oslo. The Lerone Bennett Jr. biography, *What Manner of Man,* was written, published in hard cover in record time and flown to Oslo to be presented to Dr. King by Charles Sanders for Johnson Publishing Company.

DECEMBER 1964–

I had the good fortune to accompany him to Norway when he received the Nobel Prize. Charles Sanders, later one of our managing editors, and I accompanied the party there on a two-week trip. We travelled and worked intimately with him during that period. We were the only reporter/photographer team assigned to the group, and we had a chance to get some good photographs and to get a chance to know them.

WE were in the same compartment on the train. I happened to walk through and saw Dr. King sleeping. The thing that interested me about the picture is the way he had his hands folded. There was some symbolism, as far as I'm concerned. He's sleeping very peacefully, very quietly, very calm, as I found him always to be. I don't ever remember seeing him agitated or angry about anything.

King awarded Nobel Peace Prize

KING DELIVERS SERMON in Stockholm Cathedral.

WE stopped on the way to Oslo in Stockholm for Dr. King to deliver a sermon on the anniversary of Kenyan independence. It had been raining. As I came into the courtyard, just before Dr. King got there, there was this wonderful sight of these students standing there in the rain, water dripping down their faces, with candles, singing We Shall Overcome as Dr. King moved in. This is what they had been waiting for all afternoon. It was one of the high points of the whole trip for me.

O F course, we were with Dr. King just before that evening when he received the Nobel. I took some photographs of him in his dressing room with his wife and his friend, Rev. Wyatt Walker, getting him ready. That night in the hotel room he posed for a formal photograph with his wife.

FAMILY HAS PRIVATE CELEBRATION in Oslo following the Nobel Prize ceremony.

T HEY all gravitated to Dr. King's suite at the hotel after he received the prize. So you see in the photograph, Dr. King with the medal, Coretta King with the scroll, Dr. King's mother, father, sister and brother behind him.

THIS is the moment when he received the Nobel, with all the pomp and circumstance. In addition to the medal and scroll, Dr. King received a check for $54,000, which he donated to civil rights organizations.

FUNERAL OF MALCOLM X OR EL HAJJ MALIK SHABAZZ, the Sunni Muslim name he adopted following expulsion from the Nation of Islam and his pilgrimage to Mecca. He was assassinated in New York City's Audubon Ballroom on Sunday, Feb. 21, 1965. Sleet photographed widow, Betty Shabazz, surrounded by members of Malcolm's Organization of African-American Unity, which he founded, at Unity Funeral Parlor in Harlem.

funeral of
Malcolm X

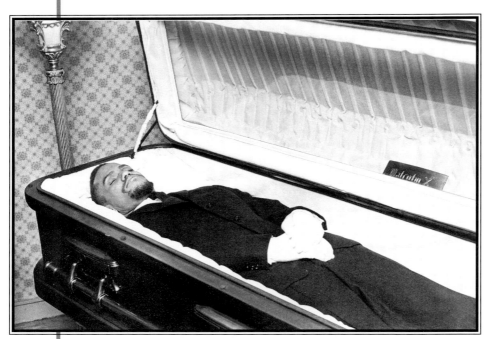

IN THIS PHOTOGRAPH HE IS IDENTIFIED AS MALCOLM X. Prior to burial he was wrapped in traditional Muslim sheets and his Islamic name displayed on the casket.

MRS. BETTY SHABAZZ and mourners at grave side.

Selma to Montgomery

I remember very vividly the fifty-mile march from Selma to Montgomery. Half of it was spent in the rain, with the military jeeps on one side, helicopters overhead and soldiers all around us.

THIS woman, marching, singing, dressed in plastic rain gear, typified what the march and the people involved in the march were all about. Here was a woman who lived in the area, who had to be there after we were long gone, and take the wrath of the people who ran the county. She is just oblivious to what is going on around her. Her singing has that determination. That is what this whole thing was all about.

THE MARCHERS WERE STOPPED BY STATE TROOPERS and county sheriffs who attempted to break up the march. When this gained national attention, the marchers gained the support of President Lyndon Johnson, who then nationalized the Alabama State Guard.

PRESIDENT *Johnson had nationalized the Alabama State Guard to provide protection for the marchers, the hated marchers from their standpoint. This particular day, I noticed this trooper, young and fit, who had been ordered to protect us. He had no choice. When the marchers would stop every now and then, he would also stop; he would walk along and stop and put his hand on his gun and look at us with what I interpreted as contempt. I said, 'Oh, boy, this would make a nice picture if I could get it.' But, I didn't want to aggravate him because that gun looked like it worked. So, he kept on. We'd stop and he'd look, and I guess I stalked him for maybe four or five miles. At one point, when he stopped and just turned, looking at us, I snapped the picture. I felt I had it.*

S ONG was used as a vital instrument to keep people galvanized during the course of the movement. During the march there were times
when it was rainy, people would become depressed, and just when the
monotony of the whole thing would begin to get to you, when spirits
would get down, someone would start a song, often a spiritual. Over here,
the gentleman with his head thrown back was Rev. James Orange of Birmingham. We called him Big Red. He had a booming bass voice, and whenever spirits would get low and we would get down, Big Red would throw
his head back and start out in this booming, wonderful voice, singing a
song. He would start singing and everybody would get up and continue
on the march as we did before. It would affect everybody, including the
photographers who were on the march.

LINE OF MARCHERS IN RAIN, showing Rev. Andrew Young (c.), with bare head and
overalls, and second from left, the Rev. James Bevel.

**IN THE MARCH, Sleet was a participant-observer. President Johnson
signed the 1965 Voting Rights bill a month after the march.**

The Freedom Summer cases lead to founding of Children's Defense Fund

MARIAN WRIGHT, Spelman College valedictorian and Yale University-trained lawyer, at age 24, with the fire of conviction burning bright, moved to Mississippi to practice law.

Under the aegis of the NAACP Legal Defense Fund, the young lawyer crisscrossed Mississippi, defending civil rights cases left in the wake of COFO's Mississippi Freedom Summer.

AFTER PASSING THE MISSISSIPPI STATE BAR, Marian Wright became the first African-American woman lawyer in Mississippi, and one of only six Black lawyers in the state. Shown here in Attorney Jack Young's Jackson office with lawyers R. Jess Brown and Carsie Hall.

ATTORNEY WRIGHT ESTIMATED that she had about 130 cases in her load, primarily school desegregation cases and those stemming from the arrests made during the height of the civil rights activities during the Summer of '64.

34

"**OUT IN THE FIELD,**" Wright (r.) talks to members of the community (l.) and is greeted by Mrs. Minnie Lewis, Dovie Hudson, and Winston Hudson of Carthage. She makes a point of seeking out those who might hesitate to bring their stories of harassment to her in Jackson.

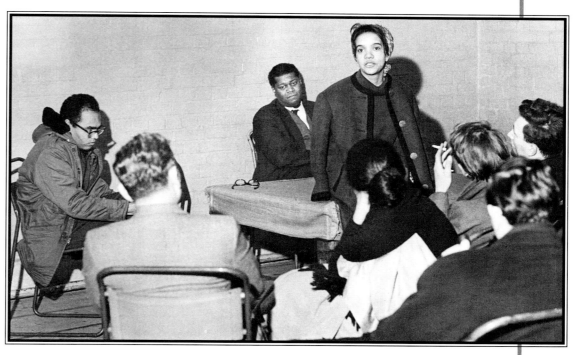

ROBERT MOSES (l.), veteran of the Mississippi Freedom Summer Project, listens as Attorney Wright discusses civil rights issues in the United States with a British Student Group against Racial Discrimination from Oxford University. The leader of the group, Dr. David Pitt, is at left behind Wright in photograph.

MARIAN WRIGHT served as secretary of The Child Development Group of Mississippi, which operated Head Start Centers throughout the state. As one of her pet projects, it set the stage for her later work with the Children's Defense Fund, a leading national advocacy organization for children's rights. Following marriage to Attorney Peter Edelman and relocating to the Northeast, she founded the fund. She is shown with (l. to r.) Martin N. Cohn, Rev. James McRee, Dan Beittel and John Mudd.

assassination of Rev. Martin Luther King, Jr., April 4, 1968

T HERE *was complete pandemonium. Nothing was yet organized because the people from SCLC were still in a state of shock. We had the world press descending upon Atlanta, plus the FBI, who were investigating the assassination.*

W E *were trying to get an arrangement to shoot in the church. They were going to pool it. Normally, the pool meant news services:* Life, Time *and* Newsweek. *When the pool was selected, there were no Black photographers from the Black media on it. Lerone Bennett and I got in touch with Mrs. King through Andy Young. She said if somebody from Johnson Publishing is not on the pool, there will be no pool.*

W E *...made arrangements with AP (the Associated Press) that they would process the black and white film immediately after the service and put it on the wire. Later, I found out which shot they sent out...The day of the funeral, Bob Johnson, the Executive Editor of* JET, *had gotten to the church and he beckoned for me and said, 'There's a spot right here.' It was a wonderful spot.*

W HAT *I noticed...this was prior to the funeral–was the little girl fidgeting there on her mother's lap. I could relate to that, being a father and having a child close to the same age. Mrs. King was sitting there, stoic and stately, but it was specifically the child who I was thinking about at the time.*

MRS. JACQUELINE KENNEDY AND SENATOR EDWARD KENNEDY

NANCY WILSON, EARTHA KITT, SAMMY DAVIS, JR., SIDNEY POITIER

EBONY PUBLISHER JOHN H. JOHNSON expresses condolences to Mrs. King.

VICE PRESIDENT HUBERT HUMPHREY, JUSTICE THURGOOD MARSHALL

HARRY BELAFONTE and wife emerge from funeral service.

DIZZY GILLESPIE in crowd at church

MULE-DRAWN CART carries coffin of Rev. Martin Luther King, Jr.

CROWD ON STREET watches as procession passes Capitol building.

ON CAMPUS OF MOREHOUSE COLLEGE where funeral service concluded, Martin Luther King, Sr. sits between his daughter, Christine, and his wife, Mrs. Alberta King, mother of Dr. Martin Luther King, Jr. Yolanda King is directly behind her grandmother.

I was glad I was working that day because if I had not been, I would have been like a lot of people, off crying somewhere. I had a job to do and I did it as best I could.

FLOWERS banked at grave side where interment took place.

39

FOLLOWING KING ASSASSINATION, SCLC regrouped under the leadership of Rev. Ralph Abernathy (second, l.), Rev. Andrew Young, Rev. Joseph E. Lowery and Stoney Cooks at SCLC headquarters in Atlanta.

CORETTA SCOTT KING, widow of Dr. Martin Luther King, Jr., and Whitney Young, National Urban League head, in conversation in Washington for Poor People's Campaign in April 1968. The campaign had been announced by Dr. M. L. King, Jr. the month before his death.

Photo by G. Marshall Wilson

JET MAGAZINE– MAY 22, 1969—"You must be joking" were the words Moneta Sleet uttered when informed that he had won the 1969 Pulitzer Prize in news feature photography for his engrossing photo of Mrs. Martin Luther King, Jr. and daughter Bernice at the April 9, 1968, funeral of the slain civil rights leader. Thus Sleet became the first Black to win the prestigious Pulitzer in the news field since its 1917 inception and the second Black in history in any area to win the award. Gwendolyn Brooks won for her poem *Annie Allen* in 1950. Sleet said later, "I knew that it was a good photograph, but I knew that there were lots of good photographs in the running. So, there's no need of my lying, I was quite happy to win the award. And my wife, Juanita, and the kids (l. to r.), Michael, Gregory and Lisa, were thrilled."

Note: Magazine features were not eligible for Pulitzer Prizes, but Moneta Sleet, Jr.'s photograph of Mrs. King and Bernice qualified because it was sent to newspapers throughout the world over the Associated Press wire.

"I ENJOY GOING TO AFRICA. I have been to Africa maybe 25 or 30 different times on assignment, particularly when the African countries South of the Sahara started becoming independent."

Moneta Sleet, Jr.

Africa and the world

IN MARCH 1957, VICE PRESIDENT AND MRS. RICHARD NIXON embarked on a 22-day goodwill tour of eight African countries and Rome, Italy. Mr. and Mrs. John H. Johnson with Moneta Sleet and Washington editor Simeon Booker represented Johnson Publishing Company. Other African-Americans on the tour were E. Frederick Morrow, administrative assistant to President Eisenhower; Claude and Etta Barnett for the Associated Negro Press; Alex Rivera, *The Pittsburgh Courier*; Louis Lautier, *The Afro American*; and Ethel L. Payne, syndicated columnist.

THE FIRST STOP WAS RABAT, MOROCCO. Vice President Nixon was greeted by Moroccan Premier M'barek Bekkai and a crowd of over 200,000 who lined the roadway from the airport into Rabat. He met with Sultan Mohammed V and Foreign Minister Ahmed Balafrej at the Royal Palace.

MRS. NIXON HOLDS two-year-old Princess Lala Amina, who was born when Sultan Mohammed V was in exile in Madagascar.

RECEPTION FOR VICE PRESIDENT NIXON in Palace at Rabat (l. to r.), the vice president spends a few minutes chatting at palace reception with Chicagoans (l. to r.), Mrs. Claude Barnett (Etta Moten), wife of Associated Negro Press (ANP) president, and Mrs. John H. Johnson (Eunice Walker Johnson) and Johnson Publishing Company and EBONY Magazine publisher John H. Johnson. Four representatives from Johnson Publishing Company covered the Nixon tour.

Ghana

THE TRIP HAD BEEN TIMED to coincide with the Independence ceremonies for the former Gold Coast, which became Ghana under Prime Minister Kwame Nkrumah. In the Cold War between East and West, the emerging African nations were being wooed by the United States and the Soviet Union. Upon arrival in the Accra, March 3, 1957, Nkrumah advised the vice president that Ghana "could never be neutral" in the "cold war."

PRIME MINISTER NKRUMAH with friends and fellow freedom fighter Komo Botsio

THE trip that will always stand out in my mind is my first experience in Ghana. When Ghana became independent, it was my first trip to Africa. That night when the Union Jack came down, it was a very tense moment. I had arrived there about an hour ahead of time. The stadium was filled with masses of people, as far as you could see. We photographers were on a truck bed, above the crowd so that we could see and photograph. At the moment in time, close to midnight, all of a sudden there was a cry from the people. Everybody just parted and stepped back, and into the stadium came Nkrumah. On either side were his two loyal lieutenants. Nkrumah proclaimed, 'At long last the battle is ended. Ghana, our beloved country, is free forever.' Talking drums carried the message to the hinterlands.

THIS, of course, was very symbolic to them; they had thrown off the shackles of the British and had become independent. And Nkrumah proceeded to give a fiery speech. Yet, one that was not so fiery that he would drive the people into doing something that they would later regret. It was a very emotional moment for me and for everyone involved. He was terrific, inspiring.

PRIME MINISTER KWAME NKRUMAH receives documents of independence.

UMBRELLA-SHADED TRIBAL CHIEFTAIN at the University of Ghana ceremonies

LADIES of the Guild of the Good Shepherd, Accra

MRS. CORETTA SCOTT KING, Vice President and Mrs. Nixon and Rev. Martin L. King, Jr. converse at Ghana Independence ceremonies.

PRIME MINISTER NKRUMAH in conversation with Congressman Adam Clayton Powell (D-N.Y.). He was among the large group of Americans who had come to see this former colony become independent.

A HIGH POINT OF GHANA'S INDEPENDENCE WEEK was the ball in the statehouse where the Duchess of Kent danced the first dance with Prime Minister Kwame Nkrumah. She was the wife of the Duke of Kent, uncle of Queen Elizabeth II of Great Britain.

PRIME MINISTER NKRUMAH and Publisher John H. Johnson shared a conversation where the new prime minister expressed his gratitude to the Black people of America for their support and the inspiration that he received from them by reading the Black press during his studies in the U.S.

Liberia

AFRICA'S OLDEST REPUBLIC was the next stop on the African tour. Many Liberians are descendants of the freed slaves taken there by the American Colonization Society in 1822 and settled near Monrovia.

VICE PRESIDENT NIXON is greeted at airport by Vice President William R. Tolbert.

LATER, Nixon met with President William V.S. Tubman, and on March 9 he presented the Liberian Navy with two Coast Guard cutters. Tubman told American reporters that Liberia, "a free enterprise nation," had recently rejected Polish offers of an economic mission and probably would reject a Soviet invitation for Tubman to visit Moscow. U.S. Ambassador to Liberia, Chicagoan Richard Jones, watches as Vice President Nixon and President Tubman examine the Coast Guard cutters.

47

Uganda

ENTEBBE, UGANDA - MARCH 10, 1957: In Uganda, Vice President Nixon told British Governor Sir Frederick Crawford that "American prestige is at stake in Liberia and U.S. aid should be increased." He said that although "Africa is a major target for Soviet penetration," communism had suffered "a very great setback" in the region following the repression of the Hungarian rebellion.

MEETING MEMBERS of the Kabaka Mutesa II's legislative Cabinet in Entebbe, Uganda, March 10, 1957.

VICE PRESIDENT NIXON reviews the reception troops in Uganda.

ETTA MOTEN BARNETT on knees examines pottery and other objects at open-air bazaar.

ETHEL L. PAYNE examines art object.

Ethiopia

THE NIXON GROUP arrived in Addis Ababa, Ethiopia, on March 11, 1957. State Department officials confirmed March 12 in Washington that Nixon had requested Ethiopian permission for construction of a U.S. military communications center and port facilities in Massawa, on the Red Sea.

EMPEROR HAILE SELASSIE of Ethiopia, whose ancestry is traced over 3,000 years to the Queen of Sheba, greets Vice President Richard Nixon upon arrival in Addis Ababa.

MR. AND MRS. JOHN H. JOHNSON are greeted by the Emperor, who departed from custom by standing level with the Americans, rather than on a raised platform.

ETTA MOTEN BARNETT shows dramatic flair in royal gardens with one of Emperor Haile Selassie's prize leopards.

A GROUP OF NEWSMEN, including Associated Negro Press President Claude Barnett and Simeon Booker, Johnson Publishing Company Washington Bureau chief, has the opportunity for briefing by Emperor Selassie and aide.

SYNDICATED COLUMNIST ETHEL L. PAYNE is greeted by the Emperor.

the Sudan

AFTER ETHIOPIA, the next stop for the Nixon group was Khartoum, the Sudan. Vice President Nixon met briefly with Sudanese Premier Abdullah Khalil and Foreign Minister Ahmed Mahgoub. In the Sudan the crowds were limited. Although the country had achieved independence January 1, 1956, it had been under martial law. Simeon Booker noted that in the Sudan, E. Fred Morrow rode in the Nixon limousine.

THE SAME AFTERNOON, Vice President Nixon visited Moslem leader Ali Al-Mirghani for tea.

TEA TIME in the Sudan found Mrs. Nixon on the right and Mr. Nixon on the left of Abdul Rahman Al-Mahdi, leader of the Ansar Moslem Sect.

THIS photograph was made in Khartoum, the Sudan. Vice President Nixon had just visited a religious leader here in this particular palace and was just leaving. As I ran down the steps, I spotted this soldier standing guard there and made this photograph, which is one of my personal favorites. An elaborate stairway, filled with rhythm and patterns, the vertical lines of the steps...make a dramatic frame for this photograph.

Libya

THE GROUP LANDED IN TRIPOLI, LIBYA, March 14, after having had engine trouble and having been forced to return to Khartoum for a new plane. Vice President Nixon cancelled a scheduled Tobruk meeting with Libyan King Idris I. But he met with Libyan Premier Mustafa Halim, who said at a dinner honoring the Nixons that the Eisenhower Doctrine was aimed at "assisting us to maintain our independence in the face of attempts to sabotage that independence." Halim urged the U.S. to aid in settlement of the Arab refugee problem and back the Algerian rebel movement.

Rome, Italy

ROME, MARCH 16-17. The Nixon tour was welcomed to Rome by Italian Premier Antonio Segni. The Vice President met with President Giovanni Gronchi and Foreign Minister Gaetano Martino.

AFTER A PRIVATE AUDIENCE WITH NIXON, Pope Pius XII praised President Eisenhower and the American people for their "expression of goodwill as a key instrument for the settlement of international disputes."

THOMAS HADDEN, 27, from Raleigh, N.C., was the only African-American student among the 260 at the North American College in Rome. He is shown with classmates (l.) Francis Gallagher of Toledo, Ohio, and (r.) Philip Magaldi of Providence, R.I. The North American College is for students training for the Roman Catholic priesthood.

THREE COINS in the Trevi Fountain at Rome

NIXON MET WITH PREMIER HABIB BOURGUIBA, and they toured Tunis in an open car. Bourguiba told reporters that he had urged the U.S. to make France aware of "the danger of continuing the atrocious war in Algeria."

Tunis

TUNISIA, MARCH 18-20
Vice President Nixon and his entourage flew to Tunis, the capital city of Tunisia, to participate in ceremonies marking the first anniversary of Tunisian independence. Independence from France had been reached by negotiation on March 20, 1956.

ENTHUSIASTIC CROWDS lined the streets to see the American vice president and give voice to their new independence. Following this visit on June 25, 1957, the Constituent Assembly ended the monarchy and declared Habib Bourguiba president.

home to the United States

MARCH 21, 1957–
Upon his return, Vice President Nixon called for settlement of the Arab refugee problem. He said it was "the cancer right in the heart of the Mid-East difficulty." He urged "higher priority" for the U.S. representation in Africa and "more effective" U.S. Information Service work in the area.

NIXON with press on plane (rear, c.), Louis Lautier, John H. Johnson and Alex Rivera.

NIXON THANKS E. Frederick Morrow, presidential administrative assistant, for his effective work on the trip. Morrow had become the first African-American named to an executive position in the White House, July 25, 1955.

Nigeria

SELF-GOVERNMENT, 1960

In October 1960 when Nigeria formed its first government as a prelude to independence, three major sections of the country were brought together under a National Parliament. The parliament was headed by the Federal Prime Minister Sir Alhaji Abubakar Tafawa Balewa, 48, former Federal Minister of Transport. It was Tafawa Balewa's job to govern the diverse sections of the large country, i.e., the predominantly Moslem North populated largely by members of the Hausa tribe; the Western region, predominantly Yoruba, headed by Chief Akintola, with a population of Christians, Moslems and those practicing native religions; and the Eastern region, primarily populated by members of the Ibo tribe. Nnamdi Azikiwe (Zik) of Ibo origins was named governor general. October 1, 1963, Nigeria became an independent republic. Azikiwe became president.

PRIME MINISTER ABUBAKAR TAFEWA BALEWA (l.) and Premier Alhaji Sir Ahmadu Bello, the Sardauna of Sokoto, share leadership of the Northern People's Congress Party. At right is Dr. Nnamdi (Zik) Azikiwe, the American-educated governor general and president of the Senate of the Nigerian Parliament.

BRITISH GOVERNOR GENERAL JAMES ROBERSON turned over affairs of state to Prime Minister Abubakar Tafawa Balewa (l.) after 31 years of Colonial Service in Africa.

SIR ABUBAKAR TAFEWA BALEWA with Johnson Publishing Company's Gerri Major and Atlanta University President Dr. Rufus Clement.

Dr. W.E.B. DuBois attends reception in Lagos at the invitation of Dr. Azikiwe and chats with U.S. Ambassador Joseph Palmer II.

ONE of my favorite photographs is this one of the jubilant teenagers in school uniforms who have come to witness the transfer of power from the British government to a Nigerian federal government.

Kenya

INDEPENDENCE CELEBRATION
NAIROBI, KENYA–DECEMBER 12, 1963

KENYATTA is dressed in a European business suit combined with a brimless African hat, decorated with the triangle pattern that symbolizes Mount Kenya. Kenyatta was born in central Kenya, but he attended college in England. His mixed costume seems to reflect the two influences that shaped his life. Prince Philip of Great Britain is seated on platform. Kenyatta is holding a silver fly whisk, a traditional symbol of power and stability in Africa. Mrs. Kenyatta (r.) is seated holding white purse.

THE activism of the newly-seated prime minister, Jomo Kenyatta, served to bring about an independent Kenya. It made him a hero among his own people.

KENYATTA IS SURROUNDED by well-wishers, among them the Mau Mau resistance fighter (c.), who holds his own fly whisk in a kind of salute.

COSTUMED TRIBAL DANCER

OGINHA ODINGA, MINISTER OF HOME AFFAIRS (l.), and Tom Mboya, minister of Justice and Constitutional Affairs and president of the Kenya Labor Union (r.), enjoy a moment of humor during the celebration of Independence or UHURU. Mboya, later heir apparent to Kenyatta and Economics Minister, was assassinated on July 5, 1969.

GIFTS FROM PRESIDENT LYNDON JOHNSON are presented to Kenyatta by Stewart L. Udall, head of the American delegation. Seated (l. to r.) are Walter Reuther, president of the UAW-CIO, Special Ambassador John H. Johnson, Udall and Kenyatta.

Liberian Inaugural

RIDING IN THE PARADE through the streets of Monrovia with the 68-year-old president was Guinea's Sekou Toure.

*P*RESIDENT *William V.S. Tubman was a very inter-esting man, very colorful and one whom I had the opportunity to photograph quite often.*

AS THE OLDEST REPUBLIC in Africa celebrated the fifth inaugural of President William V.S. Tubman, leaders of more recently independent African nations joined in the ceremonies. During the inaugural ceremony, January 6, 1964, President Tubman is at the podium while Vice President William R. Tolbert is seated behind him.

LIBERIAN SECRETARY OF LABOR, Agriculture and Commerce Stephen Tolbert and his wife, Neh Rita Singai, join the distinguished guests for the inaugural ceremonies.

DR. STEPHEN WRIGHT, former president of Fisk University, California Congresswoman Mrs. Helen Gahagan Douglas and David Rockefeller at U.S. Embassy Garden Party.

CONSUL TO LIBERIA WILLIAM JONES of Chicago and his wife greet President Tubman at garden party.

PRESIDENT TUBMAN with Raymond Firestone of Firestone Rubber Co. and UN Ambassador Nathan Barnes.

Senegal: First World Arts Festival

IN 1961, Senegal broke from Federation of Mali and declared its own independence. Leopold Senghor, the poet and father of "Negritude," won the election and became the first president of Senegal. In 1966, Senegal hosted the First World Festival of Negro Arts in Dakar under the auspices of the Senegalese government, UNESCO and the Society of African Culture.

DUKE ELLINGTON'S orchestra in open-air concert at Dakar.

U.S. AMBASSADOR TO SENEGAL MERCER COOK, Mrs. Cook and Duke Ellington at Ambassador's reception in Dakar.

ETHIOPIAN EMPEROR HAILE SELASSIE arrives for festival with host President Leopold Senghor.

PARTICIPANTS in eight-day conference represented over 30 countries and included artists and performers such as Russian poet Yevgeny Yevtushenko, American dancer Katherine Dunham, artist Hale Woodruff, Nigerian playwright Wole Soyinka and festival originator Senegal's own Alioune Diop.

A SENEGALESE WOMAN cradles her baby.

CROWD enjoys open-air concert.

AN EGYPTIAN DANCER entertains Festival participants.

A SENEGALESE MAN guides bicycle with child.

DANCERS FROM SIERRA LEONE were a festival favorite. One of the most colorful presentations was by the colorfully-costumed "Birddancer."

THE MAJESTIC GRANDEUR of the National Assembly chambers in Dakar provided the main venue for the First World Festival of Negro Arts from April 1, 1966. The twenty-six-day colloquium of conferences, performances and exhibitions on Negro Art and Culture was a culmination of ideas fomented by President Leopold Sedar Senghor (seated top, c.) and festival organizer Alioune Diop (at podium), who opened the first session. French Minister of Culture Andre Malraux is seated at Senghor's left.

NIGERIAN PLAYWRIGHT WOLE SOYINKA directed and produced his controversial drama, *Kongi's Harvest*, which deals with a paranoid dictator of an unnamed African state.

AMONG THOSE SEATED in the auditorium representing the United States are Poet Langston Hughes, Dancer Katherine Dunham and Sociologist Dr. St. Clair Drake.

MADAME SENGHOR, President Senghor and Mrs. Mercer Cook, Sr. at Ellington Concert.

FREDERICK O'NEAL, Mrs. Virginia Inness Brown, American chairman of the First World Festival, Dr. James A. Porter and Langston Hughes at reception.

PRESIDENT SENGHOR escorts French Minister of Culture Andre Malraux through exhibit hall.

DR. ROSEY POOL, Dutch-English anthologist of Black Literature, Langston Hughes, Clifford Simmons and Davidson Nicol prepare for literature workshop.

Haley returns to *Roots*

MANDINKA TRIBAL ELDERS surround Alex Haley. Kunte Kinte was a Mandinka.

ALEX HALEY returns to roots in Juffre with his brothers, architect Julius and attorney George.

I went back with Alex Haley when he made his first trip back to Africa after he had done his book, Roots. I went along with him to photograph his homecoming. I enjoyed it because it was like going back to my own roots.

MRS. BINTA KINTE FOFANA (r.) is widow of the the griot who told Haley of his relationship to Kunte Kinte, the teenager kidnapped from his village on the Gambia River and sold into slavery, who was Alex Haley's paternal ancestor on the maternal side.

THIS ODYSSEY was described in the overwhelmingly successful book *Roots*, which was made into a television miniseries. Since the book and film were part fiction as well as history, Haley's Pulitzer Prize was given in a special category.

OCK workers who were watching us just before we took the boat up river to Juffre in the Gambia.

VILLAGE CHIEF Barkary Taal welcomes the Haleys to the ancestral village of Juffre, up the Gambia River. Gambia, only 15 miles wide, is surrounded by Senegal, except at the mouth of the river.

HALEY AND BROTHERS, George and Julius, meet with Gambian President Dawda K. Jawara on the grounds of the official residence in Banjul, the capital located on the Atlantic Coast at the mouth of the River Gambia.

PORTRAIT OF MANDINKA WOMAN

THOMPSON AND SLEET JOINED JIMMY PLINTON, Trans World Airline's director of Special Markets, and Willis W. Corbett of St. Louis, demonstration consultant for Winchester Rifles, in a TWA/Winchester-sponsored safari that promoted big-game hunting in East Africa to African-American sports enthusiasts and hunters.

EBT on Safari-

OCTOBER 8, 1968, 10:30 A.M., ERA BELL THOMPSON, EBONY Magazine's International Editor, wrote:
"Seated before a typewriter in front of a green canvas tent somewhere in Northern Tanzania, I am a nervous party to what is probably the world's first all-Afro big-game hunt. "

DR. HUBERT C. HUMPHREY, New Jersey physician and sportsman, and Henry Kibiego, the first Black African to obtain a permit as a "professional" hunter, along with G. N. Macharia, the acting chief game warden, made up the hunting party. Although they tracked elephants for many miles, the huge animals eluded the hunters, as did the king of the jungle, the lion.

AT SAFARI'S END, Thompson, the lone woman on the shoot, bagged a zebra and a gazelle while Dr. Humphrey and Corbett shot wildebeest, impala and buffalo, as well numerous flying fowl.

Era Bell Thompson wrote:
"The real winner was Sleet, who with his seven cameras shot every creature in the East African kingdom."

Atlanta students in Russia

SLEET ACCOMPANIED A GROUP OF 13 STUDENTS from Atlanta's Booker T. Washington High School when they toured Russia in the summer of 1969. Ms. Bella Davis, their teacher, prepared them for the trip by tutoring them in Russian language and culture for the year prior to their departure . They were accompanied by Mrs. Elizabeth Christian, guidance teacher. Professor Arvids Zie Donis, Jr. was in charge of all academic arrangements for the group. The students who made the historic trip were Stanley Atwater, Anna Calhoun, Paula Caruthers, Janice Franklin, Glenda Gilmer, George Jeter, Jr., Freddie Johnson, Ellen Rooney, Brenda Shockley, Sandra Tolbert, Tony Williamson, Madeline Woodley and Cerri Woods.

The tour was under the sponsorship of the Citizens Exchange Corporation, a voluntary non-profit association.

STUDENTS PHOTOGRAPHED at the statue of the great Russian writer Alexander Pushkin in the Square of the Arts, St. Petersburg. Pushkin's paternal grandfather was African.

THE SUMMER PALACE at Tsarskoye Selo or the Czar's Village, not far from St. Petersburg, was built by Peter the Great and added to by his daughter, Catherine. This magnificent palace with its white columns, set against a bright blue background and gold baroque moldings, faces a spacious park with great fountain in the center. The private Royal chapel with the golden domes is on the north end of the palace. A short distance from the palace gates is the home where Alexander Pushkin lived when he was growing up and attending school on the palace grounds. During the Communist period, the village was known by Pushkin's name. Tsarskoye Selo was restored when Leningrad reverted to St. Petersburg.

STUDENTS ARRIVE in St. Petersburg aboard Scandinavian Airlines jet. In 1969 at the time of the students' visit, the city was known as Leningrad.

IN RED SQUARE students talk with Russian citizens and tourists and a Citizens Exchange Corporation button is exchanged for a piece of orange offered by the Russian worker.

O N the visit to Lenin's glass-enclosed tomb, where his body is preserved, people are scrutinized thoroughly as they file past the body. We watched the changing of the guard, and no photographs, noise or anything that would seem disrespectful was allowed. Guards explained that it was against regulations for them to take a photograph with the students, but they were included in the unposed photographs. With tough, elite guards every few feet, the guard complimented Miss Davis, the group's sponsor, on how well-behaved the students were and what an obvious zest for life they had. The guards spoke in Russian and were surprised to learn that the African-American students from the United States were Russian-language students._

THE HISTORIC LANDMARKS IN RED SQUARE in the shadow of the Kremlin and the famed onion domes of St. Basil's Cathedral as the background, Tony Williamson, George Jeter, Jr., Stanley Atwater and Glenda Gilmer are in the foreground. St. Basil's Cathedral was erected during the reign of Ivan the Terrible, 1551-1561.

GIRLS VISIT IN DORMITORY OF LENA ODIASHVILLY (center), a 17-year-old student from Siberia, who was in Moscow taking college entrance exams.

IN THE SPACE AND TECHNOLOGY PAVILION IN MOSCOW, Tony and Freddie look at the replica of the launcher that was used for the first six Russian astronauts in the Sputnik era.

TOBAGO BEACH

SURINAM SUNSET, 1973

Young's Last Mission to Africa

ANDREW J. YOUNG, civil rights worker and aide to Rev. Martin Luther King during the height of the movement, became the first African-American since the Civil War to be elected to represent Georgia's 5th Congressional District. He was re-elected twice to Congress. In 1977, at the urging of President Jimmy Carter, Young stepped down from Congress and accepted the position as U.S. Ambassador to the United Nations.

In 1979, in an attempt to delay a UN vote that was potentially embarrassing to the United States, Young had an unauthorized meeting with the UN representative of the Palestine Liberation Organization (PLO).

The resulting firestorm of criticism from the Israeli government and from some elements of the Jewish and conservative American communities caused Ambassador Young to submit his resignation to President Carter.

Prior to the resignation becoming effective, a previously scheduled eighteen-day trade mission with a twenty-five-man delegation to eight African nations was carried on. Starting in Liberia, the group continued on to the Ivory Coast, Nigeria, Cameroon, Kenya, Tanzania, Uganda and Senegal. In each country, Young and the group were given a warm reception.

Young offered assurances to the various heads of state that his departure would not affect the positive policies relating to Sub-Saharan Africa that he had helped to design.

JET Magazine's Associate Publisher Robert E. Johnson and Moneta Sleet, Jr. went along, and extensive coverage was given to the trip by both EBONY and JET magazines. Young met with the following: William Tolbert–Liberia, Alhaji Shehu Shagari–Nigeria, Julius Nyerere–Tanzania, Leopold Senghor–Senegal, Godfrey Binaisa–Uganda, Ahmadou Ahidjo–Cameroon and Aristedes Pereira–Cape Verde.

WILLIAM TOLBERT, president of Liberia, and Ambassador Young, renew old friendship.

DURING A BRIEF UNSCHEDULED stop in the Cape Verde Islands, he met briefly with President Aristedes Pereira.

IN THE IVORY COAST, the U.S. Import/Export Bank Chairman Thomas Moore, Jr (r.), Bruce Llewellyn, president, Overseas Investment, Inc (c.), and Louis Martin, special assistant to President Jimmy Carter (l.), discussed with press the importance of increasing trade with Africa. Moore reported that $250 million in private capital had been invested in the Ivory Coast. An additional $340 million construction project under the sponsorship of the Pullman-Kellogg group to build a chemical fertilizer plant was finalized.

ON THE EVE OF HIS INAUGURAL as the new Nigerian president, Alhaji Shehu Shagari and Ambassador Young met in Lagos to explore the use of Nigerian oil resources as a lever to end racism in South Africa.

AT A GOVERNMENT RECEPTION FOR THE U.S. AMBASSADOR, he was given the robes of a chieftain and the symbolic whisk of power by government officials. Ivory Coast President Houphouët-Boigny in his 19th year as president was unable to attend, but all diplomatic courtesies were observed.

YOUNG MET WITH OUTGOING PRESIDENT General Olusegun Obasanjo and chieftains from the Northern area of Nigeria.

IN THE CAMEROONS AT YAOUNDE, the capital, Young and his trade group exchange views with President Ahmadou Ahidjo (r.) and U.S. Ambassador Mabel M. Smythe flanks him on the left.

LEOPOLD SENGHOR, president of Senegal, and Ambassador Young, old friends, disagreed regarding the U.S. and Senegalese positions on Israel. While Young was seeking reconciliation between African nations and the Jewish state, Senghor stated that he would not consider restoring relations with Israel until the issue of Palestine was resolved.

YOUNG WITH KENYA PRESIDENT DANIEL ARAP-MOI, successor to the legendary Jomo Kenyatta, and U.S. aide Robert Kitchen.

UGANDA'S PRESIDENT GODFREY BINAISA meets with Ambassador Young. During the conference, Binaisa concluded a $60 million business deal with TAW President Thomas Wood.

TAW International Leasing's President Thomas A. Wood, shown with Bank Anthony, signed a $60 million deal to lease heavy machinery and transportation equipment to help market Ugandan coffee.

In Tanzania, President Julius Nyere and Young share a humorous moment when they discussed the role played by Nyere in ousting Idi Amin from Uganda.

Upon return to the United States, the group met with President Carter, who asked the departing Ambassador Young when he was going back to Africa since the mission had been such a success. Young was succeeded in the post by career diplomat Donald McHenry.

TABU production chief Clarence Avant with King Sunny Ade, a Nigerian composer and juju musician.

OTHERS IN THE TRADE MISSION were Ofield Dukes, Washington, D.C., public relations specialist; Dwayne O. Daniels of Archer-Daniels Midland Co.; Frank Delzio of Westinghouse Electric Co.; Joseph Guido of Motorola; Paolo Fresco of General Electric; Executive Vice President W. Earl Turner of Texas Independent Producers; and President DeVon R. Woodland of the National Farmers Organization.

Namibian Independence

PRESIDENT SAM NUJOMA, president of the South West African People's Organization (SWAPO) since its founding in April 1959, was sworn in as president of the New Republic of Namibia during ceremonies on March 21, 1990, in the capital city of Windhoek.

Administering the oath of office was UN Secretary-General Perez de Cuellar and witnessing the transfer of power was South African President F. W. de Klerk.

The South African Flag was lowered, and the flag bearing the national emblem of the new country was raised.

Among those present were Capetown's Archbishop Desmond Tutu and Zambia's President Kenneth Kaunda; U.S. Secretary of State James Baker and his Soviet counterpart Eduard A. Shevardnadze; PLO Chairman Yasser Arafat and Nigeria's General Ibrahim Babangida; African National Congress leader, the recently-freed Nelson Mandela, and his wife, Winnie Mandela; Dr. Betty Shabazz, the widow of Malcolm X; and Dizzy Gillespie.

Namibia was a former German colony, administered by South Africa following World War II. The United Nations rejected a request by South Africa to annex the territory in 1946, and in 1973, following years of sanctions and other rulings against the continued occupation of Namibia by South Africa, the United Nations recognized SWAPO as the legitimate representative of the Namibian people.

ARCHBISHOP DESMOND TUTU

YOUNG BLACK AND WHITE GIRLS celebrate Namibian Independence.

PRESIDENT SAM NUJOMA is greeted by South African President F. W. deKlerk.

STATELY HERRERO WOMEN in traditional Victorian garb march in Independence parade through downtown Windhoek.

WOMEN demonstrate against discrimination.

PRESIDENT NUJOMA and Rev. Jesse Jackson share ideas during Independence-week festivities.

SHANTY TOWN OF KATUTURA is the Black compound to which thousand of natives were moved in 1959 when apartheid was formally instituted, which resulted in riots and the deaths of many of Blacks when police guns were turned on them.

Ivory Coast's symbol of peace in world's largest basilica

THE BASILICA, Greco-Roman in architectural style from the time of Constantine, was the pattern for early Christian churches. In 1990 it was the largest church in the world, standing as a monument to one man's faith and also to his longevity as the president of the Ivory Coast. Enormous columns ring the basilica courtyard, filled with thousands of worshippers for the consecration mass conducted by Pope John Paul II. Although the majority of Ivorians are animists, a large number are Moslem. Houphouët-Boigny belonged to the minority population which is Christian and Roman Catholic.

PRESIDENT FELIX HOUPHOUËT-BOIGNY became president of the Ivory Coast in November 1960. The son of a wealthy chief of the Baoule people, he was the architect of what came to be known as the Ivory Coast's "Economic miracle." He reputedly paid for the Basilica with his personal funds and intended it as a "gift to God" and as a personal memorial to his own life.

Houphouët-Boigny died December 7, 1993, in Yamoussoukro, on the 33rd anniversary of the nation's independence. He was interred in the mausoleum at the Basilica.

POPE JOHN PAUL II consecrated The Basilica of Our Lady of Peace in the Ivory Coast city of Yamoussoukro, the birth place of President Felix Houphouët-Boigny, in September 1990.

MADAME MARIETHERESE HOUPHOUËT-BOIGNY, first lady of the Ivory Coast.

THIS MAGNIFICENT STRUCTURE is 489 feet at its tallest point, 37 feet taller than St. Peter's in Rome. It seats 7,000 people in an air-conditioned, acoustically-perfect space that permits musical performances without distortion. Four giant columns that support the crystal chandelier canopy above the altar house a giant, state-of-the-art speaker system. A pipeless, electronically programmed organ produces an authentic pipe- organ sound.

PIERRE FAKHOURY, Ivory Coast native of Lebanese descent, was the senior architect on the project. The stained glass windows of the Basilica depict only one Black face, that of President Houphouët-Boigny. According to Fakhoury, it is traditional in European glass-blowing for the person commissioning the work to be included among the faces that appear in the stained glass windows.

New South Africa— Mandela becomes president

ON MAY 24, 1994, African National Congress (ANC) leader and former political prisoner Nelson Mandela was sworn in as president of the Union of South Africa. The struggle against the apartheid regime that dominated South Africa for the previous half-century had come to an end. That it happened at all was historical. That it happened without civil war and major bloodshed was remarkable. A large delegation came from the United States to witness the historic moment so fraught with meaning for freedom lovers around the world.

Johnson Publishing Company, Inc. was present in the person of President and COO Linda Johnson Rice. John H. and Eunice Johnson, her father and mother, were present at the 1957 Independence ceremonies when Ghana became the first nation South of the Sahara to emerge from colonial rule. Significantly, 45 years earlier, Sleet was the photographer with Mr. and Mrs. Johnson who covered the events welcoming Ghana into the family of nations. Sleet and Lerone Bennett Jr., executive editor of EBONY Magazine, were with Mrs. Rice, the only African-Americans in the press group accompanying Vice President Albert Gore. Mrs. Hillary Rodham Clinton and the balance of the official U.S. delegation were in a second plane. The U.S. Congressional delegation travelled in a third plane. Others travelled on commercial airlines to be at the historic event.

ARRIVING AT JAM SMUTS AIRPORT in Johannesburg, South Africa, the official U.S. delegation to the South African inaugural ceremonies included (l. to r.) U.S. Ambassador and Mrs. Princeton Lyman, Vice President and Mrs. Albert Gore (rear, c.), Rev. Jesse Jackson, first lady Hillary Rodham Clinton, Secretary of Commerce Ronald H. Brown and Secretary of Agriculture Mike Espy. At airport seeking luggage, JPC President and COO Linda Johnson Rice greets Quincy Jones and the Rt. Rev. Frederick C. James, Bishop, Second District, AME Church.

THE PRESS MEETS FIRST LADY HILARY RODHAM CLINTON at Jan Smuts Airport. EBONY Executive Editor Lerone Bennett Jr. records her comments.

AFTER TAKING THE OATH OF OFFICE from Chief Justice M. M. Corbett, newly inaugurated President Nelson Mandela addresses 400-seat Parliament in the amphitheatre of the Union Building in Pretoria. This was the first Parliament to include a Black majority.

ARCHBISHOP DESMOND TUTU of the Anglican Church prays for the health of the multiracial nation. Jewish and Hindu prayers were also offered.

JUBILANT SOUTH AFRICANS celebrate the freeing of their country from the bonds of apartheid by the election of their first freely elected Parliament and president.

THE LARGE DELEGATION OF AFRICAN-AMERICANS included (l. to r.) Rep. William Gray (D-Pa.), Rep. Ron Dellums (D-Calif.), Rep. Kweisi Mfume (D-Md.), Rep. Louis Stokes (D-Ohio) and Rep. John Lewis (D-Ga.).

JPC PRESIDENT AND COO LINDA JOHNSON RICE, Mrs. Vernon Jordan and Alexis Herman, then director of the White House Office of Public Liaison, sit together for the activities.

THE FRONT ROW during the activity surrounding the inaugural events had (r. to l.) Ambassador Lyman, Mrs. Tipper Gore, Vice President Gore, Mrs. Hillary Rodham Clinton, Mrs. Lyman and Secretary of Commerce Ron Brown.

CHAIRMAN OF JOINT CHIEFS OF STAFF COLIN POWELL, Secretary of Agriculture Mike Espy, Secretary of Commerce Ronald H. Brown, Mrs. Coretta Scott King, Quincy Jones, Ed Lewis, Rep. Maxine Waters (D-Calif.), Ben Chavis, C. Delores Tucker, Rep. Carol Moseley Braun (D-Ill.), Rep. John Conyers (D-Mich.), Ernest Green, Rt. Rev. Frederick C. James and Rep. Bennie Thompson (D-Miss.) were in the amphitheatre of the main government building when the new South African flag unfurled.

UNITED STATES VICE PRESIDENT ALBERT GORE and South African President Nelson Mandela pose for Moneta Sleet, Jr.

PARTY AT THE RESIDENCE OF THE U.S. AMBASSADOR ends with hands joined and voices raised in *We Shall Overcome*. Vice President Gore, in a ceremony, "Lifting Up the Spirits," remembered W.E.B. DuBois and the African Methodist Episcopal Ministers and the African-American activists who influenced the South African struggle. Gore said, "To the United States, this transformation in South Africa has special significance...For decades, Americans agonized over the horrors of our own apartheid. And the struggle for justice in South Africa and in the United States has in many ways been one struggle."

YASSER ARAFAT stops to greet Alfre Woodard and Danny Glover, stars of the HBO film *Mandela*, based on the life of Nelson Mandela, and the film *Bopha*. In *Bopha*, Glover plays the role of a South African policeman caught between his love for his activist anti-apartheid son and his duties as a member of the South African system who is to uphold the laws of the apartheid state. They had been in the country to help "get out the vote" for the first national elections with Black participation.

"PHOTOGRAPHY IS A PART OF ME. The thing is to communicate with another human being. I try to watch and observe a person and let them reveal themselves with a gesture or a movement..."

Moneta Sleet, Jr.

politics and public figures

J. ERNEST WILKINS SR. (second r.), assistant Secretary of Labor, was the lone Black appointed by President Eisenhower to the six-member Civil Rights Commission–November 1957.

A(SA) PHILIP RANDOLPH, president, Brotherhood of Sleeping Car Porters, was elected vice president of the AFL/CIO in 1957. He organized the March on Washington movement, which led President Franklin D. Roosevelt to create the Commission on Fair Employment Practice in 1941.

JUANITA KIDD STOUT was appointed then elected in November 1959 as Municipal Court Judge in Philadelphia. Judge Stout, former assistant to Federal Judge William H. Hastie, at 36, became the first Black woman on the bench in Pennsylvania and one of the youngest in the nation.

89

ATTORNEY FRANK REEVES AND SENATOR JOHN F. KENNEDY in New York City at the National Conference on Constitutional Rights and American Freedom. Kennedy was the 1960 Democratic candidate for President of the United States. Reeves was the Democratic National Committeeman for Washington, D.C.

IN JUNE 1961 LESTER GRANGER, National Urban League executive director since 1941, announced his retirement from the League. Whitney Young, Jr., former Dean of the Atlanta University School of Social Work, was named as his successor. During Granger's tenure at the League, it grew from 41 to 63 branches, and its annual budget moved from $600,000 a year to $4,500,000. The League was in the forefront as it stimulated young people to seek careers in scientific and technical arenas with its Pilot Placement Program.

JANUARY 3, 1961, ADAM CLAYTON POWELL, JR. became chairman of the House of Representatives Committee on Education and Labor. He was the second Black to chair a major committee of the House. William L. Dawson (D-Ill.) became the Chair of the House Committee on Government Operations in the Truman Administration in January 1949. Photo was taken at the May 1957 Prayer Pilgrimage in Washington, D.C., which was a prelude to the 1963 March on Washington and marked the first time, labor, the Black church and civil rights organizations such as the NAACP formed an alliance.

FRANKLYN H. WILLIAMS (right, c.) was named by President Lyndon B. Johnson on October 2, 1964, as an alternate delegate to the U.S. delegation for the 1964 session of the United Nations General Assembly. Williams, a former Peace Corps official, was confirmed as Ambassador to Ghana in 1965 after appointment by President Johnson. In 1970 he became president of the Phelps-Stokes Fund, a philanthropy organized to aid in improving education for American Blacks, Native Americans and Africans.

DR. ROBERT C. WEAVER was named Secretary of the Department of Housing and Urban Development on January 13, 1966. He was unanimously confirmed and sworn in on January 18, 1966.

NOV. 8, 1966, EDWARD W. BROOKE (R-Mass.) was elected to the U.S. Senate and became the first Black to sit in that body since Reconstruction. He is shown with Massachusetts Lt. Governor Francis Sargent, his mother, Mrs. Helen Brooke, and Massachusetts Governor John A.Volpe.

91

Thurgood Marshall takes a bride–December 1955

THURGOOD MARSHALL, special counsel to the NAACP, was married to Hawaiian native Cecelia Suyat in a private ceremony at St. Philips Episcopal Church in New York City. Marshall, 47, was a widower, and Miss Suyat, 28, was secretary to Gloster Current, director of NAACP Branches. JET Magazine was given an exclusive to cover the wedding reception attended by a few close friends and associates of the couple.

MR. AND MRS. THURGOOD MARSHALL

FORMER UNITED NATIONS DELEGATE Charles Mahoney and Mrs. Norma Marshall, the groom's mother, toast the happy couple.

FEDERAL JUDGE WILLIAM HASTIE and wife, Beryl, with the couple. Roy Wilkins, behind Mrs. Hastie at right, gave the bride away.

EN ROUTE TO THE U.S. VIRGIN ISLANDS where they honeymooned, the Marshalls are photographed at Pan Am airways counter in New York.

AUGUST 30, 1967. U.S. Solicitor General Thurgood Marshall was confirmed by the U.S. Senate as Associate Justice of the United States Supreme Court. On July 13, 1965, he was named by President Lyndon B. Johnson as the Solicitor General of the U.S. Marshall was the first African-American named to the U.S. Supreme Court.

the Kennedys and the Houphouët-Boignys

PRESIDENT AND MRS. FELIX HOUPHOUËT-BOIGNY of the Ivory Coast accepted the invitation of President and Mrs. John F. Kennedy to come to the United States for a State visit in May 1962. Upon arrival in New York they were breakfast guests of Ambassador to the United Nations, Adlai Stevenson, then given a ticker tape parade up Broadway. Arriving in Washington, they were met by President and Mrs. Kennedy, Secretary of State and Mrs. Dean Rusk and other dignitaries. The official Ivory Coast delegation included Finance Minister Raphael Saller, Agriculture Minister Charles Donwaki and Supreme Court President Ernest Boka.

RED CARPET AND ROSES greeted the distinguished couple from the Ivory Coast, when President and Mrs. Kennedy and Secretary of State and Mrs. Dean Rusk met them at the Washington, D.C., airport.

WHITE HOUSE GUESTS OF HONOR and the hosts pose for formal portrait with Ivory Coast Chief Justice Ernest Boka behind President Houphouët-Boigny, Mrs. Rusk and Secretary of State Dean Rusk behind President Kennedy.

MRS. JOHN H. JOHNSON renews her acquaintance with Madame Houphouët-Boigny at luncheon hosted by Mrs. Robert Kennedy (c.), wife of the Attorney General. The two women met earlier when Publisher Johnson was Special Ambassador to the Ivory Coast for Independence Anniversary ceremonies.

MADAME HOUPHOUËT-BOIGNY AND MRS. ERNEST BOKA examine Baoule Dancing mask, which was part of a West African Art Exhibit at the U.S. Department of State. Both President and Mrs. Houphouët-Boigny were members of the Ivory Coast's Baoule tribe. She spoke French and her native language, but not English.

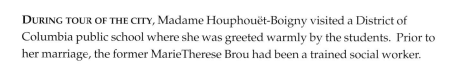
DURING TOUR OF THE CITY, Madame Houphouët-Boigny visited a District of Columbia public school where she was greeted warmly by the students. Prior to her marriage, the former MarieTherese Brou had been a trained social worker.

The Emperor of Ethiopia visits United Nations and New York City

HIS EXCELLENCY, HAILE SELASSIE, EMPEROR OF ETHIOPIA

IN 1963, HAILE SELASSIE, Emperor of Ethiopia, visited New York and the United Nations. He stayed at the Plaza Hotel where this formal portrait was made.

WITH royalty you have to be very precise. We had talked with his aide-de-camp. He wanted to know exactly where I wanted the Emperor to stand. So, I marked the spot and we waited. Not very far from the appointed time, there was this hush. He walked out to the mark we had set. I had my lights all set up. He stood there. He put his hands as you see them there. He looked at me and nodded as if to say, 'Can we take the picture? This is it! How much better can it get?' And he was right. He made the picture with his hands and with his piercing eyes.

IN AN ADDRESS TO THE 18TH SESSION of the United Nations General Assembly, Emperor Selassie reminded the world of the lessons that Africans can teach.

THAT until the Philosophy that holds one race superior and another inferior is finally and permanently discredited and abandoned...That until that day, the dream of lasting peace and world citizenship and the rule of international morality will remain but a fleeting illusion, to be pursued, but never attained.

HAILE SELASSIE

IN TICKER TAPE PARADE, the Ethiopian monarch walks five blocks to New York City Hall. Enthusiastic crowds line the route.

SINGER MIRIAM MAKEBA, a voluntary exile from South Africa, was among the guests who greeted the Emperor at New York City Hotel reception.

AT CITY HALL RECEPTION, New York City Mayor Robert F. Wagner introduced Emperor Selassie to Manhattan Borough President and former Ambassador to Liberia Edward Dudley.

MRS. ANGIER BIDDLE DUKE, wife of the U.S. Chief of Protocol, and Ethiopian Princess Ruth Desta in receiving line at City Hall reception.

Independent African Nations at the UN

FROM FEBRUARY 1964 when Alex Quaison-Sackey of Liberia presided as the first African President of the United Nations General Assembly until the fall of 1969 when it was again Africa's turn to hold the yearlong presidency of the international organization, 32 non-White African nations took their seats in the 110-seat assembly. The president of the 1969-1970 session was Angie Brooks, lawyer, former Liberian Assistant Secretary of State and 15-year veteran of assembly participation by Liberia, Africa's oldest republic.

AFRICAN DIPLOMAT arrives at United Nations headquarters in chauffeured limousine.

REPRESENTATIVES from many of the newly independent African nations descend escalator and stairs as they make their way to opening meeting of the United nations 17th General Assembly.

ALEX QUAISON-SACKEY of Ghana in discussion with another representative.

MRS. JEANNE MARTIN of Guinea reads report prior to opening of United Nations General Assembly. Representative of Republic of Haiti is at her right.

AT THE 24TH ANNUAL SESSION of the United Nations
General Assembly in September 1969, Angie E. Brooks,
Liberia's Assistant Secretary of State, was elected without
opposition. She was the Assembly's second woman president and was the second from a West African nation.

IN LIMOUSINE she checks with aide Daniel McAleese regarding the day's schedule.

DENMARK'S AMBASSADOR HERMAN LANNING and Liberia's Angie
Brooks pause on way to 17th General Assembly meeting in 1962.

READY FOR THE WORKING DAY, President Angie Brooks, greets a colleague
during a break in the proceedings.

UN PRESIDENT ANGIE BROOKS leaves her residence in
Manhattan's Plaza Hotel for work at the United Nations.

Women move to the Federal Bench and Halls of Congress...

CONSTANCE BAKER MOTLEY, former NAACP counsel, was confirmed August 30, 1966, as U.S. District Judge in southern New York and became the first Black woman named to the federal bench.

SHIRLEY CHISHOLM, (D-N.Y.) won a seat in Congress on November 5, 1968, from Brooklyn's Bedford-Stuyvestant section by defeating Civil Rights activist and leader of CORE James Farmer. She became the first African-American woman elected to a Congressional seat.

YVONNE BRATHWAITE BURKE (D-Calif.) and Barbara Jordan (D-Texas) were elected to the U.S. Congress in November 1972. Their election added strength to the Black presence on Congressional committees. Brathwaite Burke was first Black woman to co-chair a national political convention at the 1972 Democratic National Convention. Jordan keynoted the National Democratic Convention in 1976 and was a key member of the Judiciary Committee in the Watergate hearings.

...and to City Halls

My assignment was simply to follow (Mayor Kelly) around and document what was going on with her and not disturb her as much as possible. There again, to kind of be like a fly on the wall. Hopefully, there would be some photogenic situations. It is not the easiest story in the world to do. Just hope that you have a personality that is dynamic and will offer opportunities for you to get some decent photographs. Of course, the mayor is dynamic. She is very photogenic, so that helps quite a bit.

CARRIE SAXON PERRY broke into City Hall by being elected mayor of Hartford, Conn., and was the first Black woman mayor of a major northeastern city in November 1987. Perry previously served in the State legislature.

SHARON PRATT KELLY, lawyer and former utility executive, was elected Washington, D.C., mayor in 1990. She became the first Black woman mayor of a major U.S. city.

NAACP EXECUTIVE SECRETARY ROY WILKINS places the Spingarn Medal around Sammy Davis, Jr.'s neck during presentation in December 1968 for Davis' "superb and multifaceted talent" and his contributions to the Civil Rights Movement.

LT. GOVERNOR DOUGLAS WILDER was elected governor of the State of Virginia in 1989 and became the first African-American governor of a State since the Civil War. Wilder is shown with his daughter, Loren, at the State House.

MARCH 8, 1971–BENJAMIN L. HOOKS, Memphis minister and lawyer, was named by President Richard Nixon to a seven-year term on the Federal Communications Commission. He was the first African-American named to the regulatory agency, and his appointment signalled a new awareness of the importance of minority participation in all areas of the broadcast and telecommunications industry. When his term expired at the FCC, Hooks became head of the National Association for the Advancement of Colored People (NAACP).

VERNON JORDAN, executive director of the United Negro College Fund, is named to succeed Whitney M. Young, Jr., National Urban League Executive Director on June 15, 1971. Young drowned while swimming in Lagos, Nigeria.

APRIL 28, 1971, SAMUEL LEE GRAVELY, JR. became the first African-American Admiral in the United States Navy. He was commanding officer of the *USS Roanoke,* which was docked in Portland Harbor for the city's Rose Festival. Admiral Gravely, who assumed command of the U.S. Third Fleet in 1976, gave Oregon Governor Robert Stroud an inspection tour of the ship.

achievers...

CARL T. ROWAN, former ambassador to Finland and director of the United States Information Agency during the Johnson Administration, signs copies of his 1974 book, *Just Between Us*, for Federal Communications Commissioner Benjamin Hooks. Washington Bureau editor Fannie Granton is behind Hooks in the line.

ON OCTOBER 17, 1969, Dr. Clifton Wharton, Jr. was elected President of Michigan State University and became the first Black academician to head a major predominantly White university in the 20th century. In 1978, Wharton later became chancellor of the State University system of New York and served as a member of the Board of the Rockefeller Foundation. He served briefly as Undersecretary of State in the Clinton Administration.

DR. DAVID SATCHER was installed as the eighth President of Meharry Medical College in Nashville, Tenn., on October 4, 1982. Meharry had educated more than 40 percent of the Black physicians and dentists practicing in the United States in 1982. Satcher, considered an expert in the study of sickle cell anemia, later served as director of the Center for Disease Control and Prevention and was confirmed in 1998 as Surgeon General of the United States.

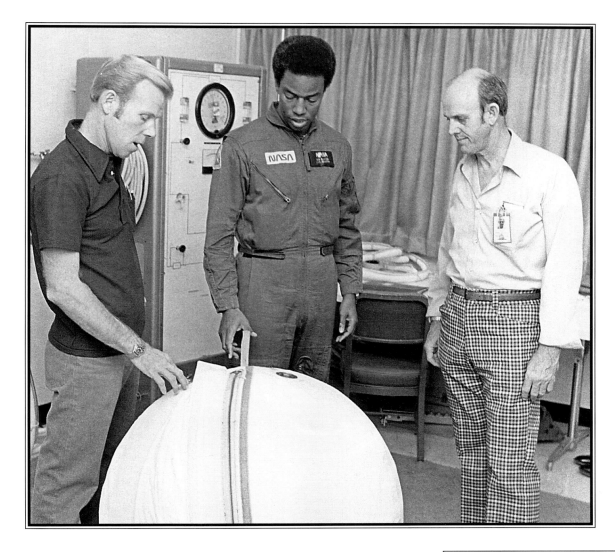

Lt. Col. Guion S. Bluford, a crew member of the space shuttle *Challenger*, became the first Black astronaut to go into outer space in 1983. He is shown with NASA staff Clyde Richardson and George Post.

On January 28, 1986, the Space Shuttle *Challenger* exploded 73 seconds after lift-off. Dr. Ronald McNair, 35, a Black physicist who held a B.S. from North Carolina A & T and a Ph.D. in Physics from MIT, was killed with six other astronauts and a civilian schoolteacher, Christa McAuliff. McNair held five regional black belt championships in Karate, and in a 1979 Ebony story, demonstrated his expertise in the martial arts.

achievers...

IN 1996, after two decades in Europe, Clotye Murdoch Larsson, former associate editor for EBONY magazine, returned to the United States and the South. During the Civil Rights Movement, she covered many stories, including the Emmett Till trial. Meeting again with movement leader Aaron Henry in his pharmacy in Clarksdale, Miss., Larsson interviewed him about the changes that had taken place during her absence. Henry, who served as NAACP president and was also one of the first African-Americans elected to the Mississippi State legislature in the post-Reconstruction, was a rich source for her research. He is shown here with Larrson in his Clarksdale drugstore where movement memorabilia line the walls and counters.

REUBEN V. ANDERSON, 42, University of Mississippi Law School graduate and circuit court judge in Jackson, Miss., was appointed in 1985 by Governor Bill Allain to a seat on the bench of the Mississippi Supreme Court. He became the first African-American to sit on the Court. When the term to which he had been appointed expired, he was elected to a regular term in November 1986. He is shown with Judge Michael Sullivan.

CAROL MOSELEY BRAUN, a Democrat from Illinois, became the first Black woman ever elected to the United States Senate when she defeated her Republican opponent 55 percent to 45 percent in the November 1992 elections. Moseley Braun served as Recorder of Deeds for Cook County (Ill.) and put together a coalition of Black and female voters that proved unbeatable. She is shown in this photo with Georgia Representative John Lewis (r.) and New York Mayor David Dinkins during the celebration of Nelson Mandela's election as President of South African in 1994.

achievers...

RONALD BROWN was the first African-American Secretary of Commerce and the first African-American of either major political party to serve as chairman. He was also the first Black partner of the law firm Batton Boggs and Blow in Washington, D.C., one of the major national lobbying law firms. As chairman of the Democratic National Committee, he was responsible for organizing the successful 1992 Democratic Convention that nominated Governor William Clinton for president. Brown was killed on April 3, 1996, when the plane in which he and thirty-four others were traveling on a trade mission to Bosnia went off-course in a thunderstorm and crashed into a mountain as the plane approached the airport at Dubrovnik. Brown, with his wife, the former Alma Arrington, their son, Michael Arrington, and daughter, Tracey Lyn, was memorialized at the 1996 Democratic National Convention.

GENERAL COLIN POWELL, Chairman of the Joint Chiefs of Staff, reviewed the troops of the Joint Service Honor Guard at the ceremony welcoming him as the new Chairman of the Joint Chiefs of Staff in Ocotber, 1989. He is accompanied by Secretary of Defense Dick Cheyney, on the Parade Field in front of the River Entrance to the Pentagon. Powell served on active duty in Vietnam, and earned the Purple Heart for wounds incurred there. He also holds the Presidential Medal of Freedom and four Distinguished Service medals. During the Iran-Contra crisis, Powell served as Deputy National Security Advisor. He was President Ronald Reagan's adviser on National Security matters for the last two years of that Administration. He was named Chairman of the Joint Chiefs by President George Bush in 1989. At 52, Powell was the youngest man to chair the Joint Chiefs of Staff and the most Junior in rank.

"THE ONE THING THAT MOVES ME AS A PHOTOGRAPHER is the freedom to be able to work. I have been fortunate to be a part of documenting not only Black America, but Black conditions in the world. I am fortunate that it has never been like work."

Moneta Sleet, Jr.

celebrations and inaugurals

20 Years of EBONY Magazine celebrated

AN ENORMOUS BIRTHDAY CAKE surrounded with roses and ribbons celebrated the 20th Anniversary of the publication of EBONY Magazine. It was the centerpiece of the celebration at the Waldorf Astoria Hotel's Starlight Room in New York City– November 29, 1965. Among the eight hundred invited guests were industry leaders, advertising executives and celebrities from stage, screen, sports, music, politics, social welfare and civil rights. As TV personality Ed Sullivan said, it was "the greatest show going on anywhere in the world." The John H. Johnsons gave a party, and everybody came.

JACKIE ROBINSON, Mrs. John H. Johnson, Jim Brown, Sammy Davis, Jr., and Publisher and CEO John H. Johnson with EBONY's 20th anniversary birthday cake.

THURGOOD MARSHALL, Publisher Johnson, Lena Horne and Arthur Godfrey at 20th Anniversary centerpiece cake.

SINGER MABEL MERCER and actress Diana Sands in forefront with Howard Beard, Lucien Happensberger, Diana Sands' husband, and Cathy White, New York *Amsterdam News* columnist.

1945 EBONY 1965

CLIFFORD ALEXANDER (c.), deputy Special Assistant to the President, brought greetings from President Lyndon B. Johnson. Vice President Hubert Humphrey's specially made film to congratulate EBONY was screened for the assembled guests during the luncheon program. New York editor Allan Morrison is at left and Publisher Johnson is right.

SAMMY DAVIS, JR. is challenged by Heavyweight champion Muhammad Ali as the two entertain luncheon guests.

MRS. GERTRUDE JOHNSON WILLIAMS, mother of Publisher John H. Johnson, and Mrs John H. Johnson laugh with Lena Horne.

ACTRESS HILDA SIMMS and U.S. Solicitor General Thurgood Marshall enjoy luncheon repartee.

MRS. CAB CALLOWAY, JPC Vice President Leroy Jeffries, UN Ambassador Dr. James M. Nabrit, Jr. and Cab Calloway share observations on the occasion.

TIME, INC. Executive and former UNCF head William Trent praises the publisher and the contributions to the community by EBONY Magazine.

FOYER DISPLAY of advertising pages in EBONY magazine demonstrates historic breakthrough to major advertising accounts by Johnson Publishing Company, Inc. The display is eagerly viewed by guests prior to luncheon program. Among them, Howard Woods (r.), associate director, U.S.I.A., George Schuyler, columnist, *Pittsburgh Courier* (c.), and Ethel Payne, syndicated columnist (front, r.).

PIANIST HAZEL SCOTT is greeted by Publisher Johnson as she arrives for 20th Anniversary luncheon.

American Black Achievement Awards

EBONY MAGAZINE continued the tradition of honoring Black Achievement that it started in 1980. The American Black Achievement Awards for 1983 were up to the standard of excellence set in previous years.

ON STAGE WITH PUBLISHER AND MRS. JOHN JOHNSON are awardees, editors and special guests. Among them, Ella Fitzgerald, Benjamin Hooks, Los Angeles Mayor Tom Bradley, who received the Martin Luther King, Jr. Public Service Award, Muhammad Ali, Dick Gregory, Rev. George H. Clements, Larry Holmes, Rev. Jesse Jackson, NAACP's Margaret Bush Wilson and Johnson Publishing Company's Senior Editor Lerone Bennett Jr., Executive Editor Herbert Nipson and Managing Editors Hans Massaquoi and Charles L. Sanders.

JOHN H. JOHNSON, publisher and CEO, announces award for Lifetime Achievement to Ella Fitzgerald.

GLADYS KNIGHT AND THE PIPS provided their own brand of outstanding achievement as they entertained the audience gathered for the awards.

ELLA FITZGERALD responds to presentation of award by Publisher Johnson.

CO-HOSTS DEBBIE ALLEN, popular choreographer, dancer and television personality, and Charles Dutton, actor, provide humor as well as emcee the show, which was taped for national television viewing.

MAE JEMISON (second, l.), the first African-American woman astronaut, awaits her call to the stage for the Trail Blazer Award. Illinois Senator Carol Moseley Braun was also given the Trail Blazer Award for being the first African-American woman in the United States Senate. U.S. Representative Maxine Waters received the Public Service Award while Joe Williams received the award for Lifetime Achievement.

IN THE YEAR OF THE 50TH ANNIVERSARY of the company's founding, Johnson Publishing Company hosts the 14th Annual Black Achievement Awards–November 8, 1992, at the Aquarius/Star Search Theatre in Hollywood. The American Black Achievement Awards was the only televised program that recognized Black Americans for achievement in Athletics, Arts, Sciences, Public Service and Humanities.

CARMEN McRAE accepts the Music Award for another jazz legend and close friend, Dizzy Gillespie, whose illness did not permit him to attend.

ASSEMBLED ON STAGE FOLLOWING THE FILMING OF THE PROGRAM, the Johnson Publishing Company corporate family, including Publisher and Mrs. John H. Johnson, Mrs. Linda Johnson Rice, Lerone Bennett. Jr,. executive editor, EBONY Magazine, Robert E. Johnson, executive editor and associate publisher, JET Magazine, Herbert Temple, art director, Sylvia Flanagan, JET senior editor, Hans Massaquoi, Simeon Booker, Washington Bureau Chief, and other guests.

inaugural sampler

MONETA SLEET, JR. was a part of the cadre of Johnson Publishing Company staff who covered the activities surrounding the inaugurals of presidents and vice presidents of the United States. A sampler of Sleet coverage of inaugural activities over the years follows:

1965–DEMONSTRATORS seeking Home Rule for the District of Columbia parade before reviewing stand while President Lyndon B. Johnson and Vice President Hubert Humphrey and their wives observe. They were later joined by the NAACP's Roy Wilkins, the National Urban League's Whitney Young and Ralph Bunche, undersecretary of the United Nations.

CAROL BURNETT, Harry Belafonte and Julie Andrews rehearse for gala.

MRS. GERTRUDE JOHNSON WILLIAMS and Ponchitta Pierce, EBONY Associate editor, meet Mrs. Hubert Humphrey at Distinguished Ladies Reception.

SINGER-COMPOSER OSCAR BROWN, JR. and wife, Maxine (l.), are with friends at Sheraton Park Inaugural Ball.

OPERA STAR MARIAN ANDERSON proceeds through receiving line at Distinguished Ladies Reception. Mrs. Dean Rusk is at her left.

the first Nixon inaugural–1969

JANUARY 20, 1969–LIONEL HAMPTON at Kennedy Center Inaugural Ball. The theme of the Inaugural was *Forward Together*.

MR. AND MRS. JOHN H. JOHNSON, boxholders at the Inaugural Ball in the D.C. Hilton, are joined by their guests, Mr. and Mrs. Earl B. Dickerson and Dr. and Mrs. William Walker. Dickerson was President of Supreme Life Insurance Company of Chicago. Dr. Walker is Mrs. Johnson's brother.

the second Nixon inaugural 1973

TWO OF THE FIVE THOUSAND BLACKS who participated in the activities surrounding the second Nixon Inaugural, this couple clearly enjoy the music and put feeling into the dance.

BROOKLYNITES COLONEL AND MRS. WILLIAM A. ROBERTS join the revelers at the Inaugural Ball in the Washington Hilton. Colonel Roberts, in full dress uniform, was with the Brooklyn Army Terminal.

1973 SECOND -NIXON INAUGURAL JOHN WILKS (c.), Black member of the Nixon Inaugural Committee, escorts Mrs. Patricia Nixon and Mrs. Julie Eisenhower through tour of the Corcoran Gallery's exhibit and the reception.

Georgia's Jimmy Carter signals a New South

IN PRE-ELECTION strategy session, Atlanta Mayor Maynard Jackson and candidate Jimmy Carter share ideas.

NOVEMBER 1976–At the Inaugural Parade seated in the Presidential Box are Mrs. Carter, President Carter, Vice President and Mrs. Walter Mondale. Sleet, always with his photographer's eye for the child, catches Amy Carter, the president's young daughter, who has her own special view from a space on the lower level.

INTEGRATED FLOAT from AFL-CIO Building Trades at Carter-Mondale 1977 Inaugural.

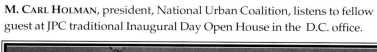
VICE PRESIDENT MONDALE collides with supporter at crowded reception.

AT LINCOLN MEMORIAL SERVICE, Rev. M. L. King, Sr. reminds his listeners that they must not forget the Dream or the Dreamer.

M. CARL HOLMAN, president, National Urban Coalition, listens to fellow guest at JPC traditional Inaugural Day Open House in the D.C. office.

MR. AND MRS. JOHN H. JOHNSON and Supreme Life Insurance President and Mrs Ray Irby.

The Reagan–Bush/ Bush–Quayle Years, 1981-1993
First Reagan Inaugural, 1981

PRESIDENT-ELECT RONALD REAGAN and Vice President George Bush with the assembled VIPs stand as Juanita Booker of Paso Robles, Calif., sings *The Star Spangled Banner* at the inaugural ceremony.

SAMUEL PIERCE, named by President-elect Reagan to the position of Secretary of the Department of Housing and Urban Development, is with his wife at the Reagan-Bush Inauguration.

AT THE FIRST REAGAN INAUGURAL, Mrs. and Mrs. John H. Johnson, and their daughter, Linda with her escort, Eugene Dibble and brother Andrew Dibble, at the Smithsonian Museum Inaugural Ball. The Johnson family has attended every inaugural since the Eisenhower Administration and has hosted an Open House in the Washington, D.C., offices of Johnson Publishing Company, Inc.

FELLOW CHICAGOANS W. CLEMENT STONE and the First National Bank's Hamilton Talbert celebrate the Republican victory and discuss the outlook for business under the new administration.

The Second Reagan Administration

THE SECOND REAGAN ADMINISTRATION began with arctic weather and what was noted as a concerted effort on the part of African-American members of the Administration to bridge what they perceived as a growing gap between the administration and their communities. The traditional outdoor swearing-in ceremony was transferred into the Capitol Rotunda because of the inclement weather, and the usual parade down Pennsylvania Avenue to the White House was also cancelled.

HAPPILY, THE REAGANS greet their supporters at one of the many Inaugural Balls and thank them for their support.

LIONEL HAMPTON, a long-time Reagan supporter, took time out of an engagement to perform at Inaugural Ball.

CHICAGO ATTORNEY JEWEL LAFONTANT and son John Rogers at Inaugural Ball. Lafontant was from a prominent Chicago Republican family and served as first Black woman Assistant Attorney General in the Eisenhower Administration.

SAMMY DAVIS, JR., in his trademark performance, entertains the audience.

THE 50TH AMERICAN PRESIDENTIAL INAUGURAL BLACK
COMMITTEE AWARDS were made to John H. Johnson, publisher
of EBONY Magazine, for the Corporate sector by Dr. Gloria E.A.
Toote, vice chair of the President's Advisory Council on Private
Sector initiatives. The Award for Community Leadership was
given to Lou Rawls, who performed at the Presidential gala, by
Robert Brown, High Point, N.C., businessman and special assistant
for liaison with minority groups in the Nixon Administration. Dr.
James Cheek, president of Howard University, was given the
award for Education by Kaaren P. Johnson for the Committee.
HUD Secretary Samuel R. Pierce was given the award for
Government. The presentations were made at a luncheon held on
the campus of the University of the District of Columbia.

DR. GLORIA E.A. TOOTE, JOHN H. JOHNSON AND ROBERT BROWN

LOU RAWLS AND ROBERT BROWN

DR. GLORIA TOOTE, KAAREN P. JOHNSON AND
DR. JAMES CHEEK

JOHN WILKS (l.) was a member of the Black Republican Council of 100 and a member of the Bush team since the 1980 election of the vice president on the Reagan-Bush ticket.

GENERAL AND MRS. JULIUS JOHNSON at gala during Bush-Quayle inaugural. General Johnson was deputy chairman of the Inaugural Military Committee.

LIONEL HAMPTON, often the entertainer for the Republican inaugural celebrations, headed the National Black Republican Council gala for the Bush inaugural. He is shown here under the tent at a special Hamp At The White House in the Reagan–Bush years.

ENTERTAINER PEARL BAILEY joins Hampton in program.

Second New South Governor Inaugurated as President, William Jefferson Clinton–

January 20, 1993

At left, kicking off the five days of Inaugural activity, the Clintons join hands with the community as they cross the Memorial Bridge. The Reunion on the Mall was one of the highlights of the Clinton-Gore Inaugural.

Below, Maya Angelou reads *On the Pulse of Morning*, her poem written for the inaugural.

Below, Mr. and Mrs. Vernon Jordan greet friends at the Clinton-Gore inaugural ceremony. Jordan, former National Urban League executive, headed President Clinton's Transition Team.

Newly inaugurated President William Jefferson Clinton, daughter Chelsea and first lady Hillary Rodham Clinton wave to the crowd. Vice President Albert Gore (r.) joins in applause.

Maya Angelou, whose commissioned poem, *On the Pulse of Morning*, opened the inaugural ceremonies, is the center of this group of admiring friends (l. to r.): Representative Maxine Waters (D-Calif.), Spelman College President Johnnetta Cole, actress Cicely Tyson and White House Liaison Alexis Herman.

MR. AND MRS. JOHN H. JOHNSON, publisher and CEO, Johnson Publishing Co., Inc., and daughter, Linda Johnson Rice, JPC president and COO, pose with South African leader Nelson Mandela during Gala.

THESE PARTY-GOERS are a few of the estimated 50,000 African-Americans who made their way to Washington to celebrate the new administration. They formed a strong line for the Democrats.

WYNTON MARSALIS blows his trumpet to signal a good new day.

DOROTHY HEIGHT, president of the National Council of Negro Women, and Ernest Green, the first Black graduate of Arkansas' Little Rock Central High School, meet at one of the inaugural receptions. Green served as assistant Secretary of Labor in the Carter Administration and was later named by Clinton to serve as Chairman of the Board of the African Development Foundation.

PHOTOGRAPHER-AUTHOR-FILM DIRECTOR GORDON PARKS SR. and Democratic National Committee Chair Ron Brown greet each other at one of the black-tie events.

"**THE ONE THING THAT MOVES ME AS A PHOTOGRAPHER**, and I think it is so important to any photographer or any photojournalist, is the freedom to be able to work...With me, in particular, how important my whole family life has been for me. I have been fortunate enough to have that in my wonderful wife and children. Parents, too, who have really aided me. You know, we do none of this alone."

Moneta Sleet, Jr.

families – food – fashion

FOUR YEARS AFTER THE MURDER of Dr. Martin Luther King, Jr., Sleet visited the family in the Kings' Atlanta home.

MRS. KING AND BERNICE have an eyeball-to-eyeball moment. The boys play with the hoop and basketball in the backyard as Bernice watches.

THE MARTIN LUTHER KING, JR. FAMILY in front of the King Center, 28 years after the death of Rev. Dr. Martin Luther King, Jr. (l. to r.): Dexter, Yolanda, Mrs. Coretta Scott King, Bernice and Martin III.

MRS. BETTY SHABAZZ AND FAMILY, 1969

MRS. JAMES MEREDITH AND TWIN SONS, JAMES AND JOSEPH—1968

DICK GREGORY WITH FAMILY, 1977.

EARTHA KITT AND DAUGHTER KITT MCDONALD

GEOFFREY HOLDER
AND WIFE, DANCER
CARMEN
DELAVALLADE, WITH
THEIR SON, LEO

JEANNE MOUTOUSSAMY ASHE AND DAUGHTER CAMERA

PATTI LABELLE AND SON ZURI

IMAMU AMIRI BARAKA WITH FAMILY

NAT KING COLE AND TALLULAH BANKHEAD

NATALIE COLE receives a Grammy Award for her remixed version in duet form of *Unforgettable*, one of her father's hit songs.

BILL AND CAMILLE COSBY celebrate 30 years of marriage and close family ties with an elegant sit-down dinner in their New York town house in January 1994. Camille Hanks Cosby (l.) is with son, Ennis, and eldest daughter, Erika. Ennis was killed in a California highway robbery in 1997. At right Camille Cosby is seated, and Bill Cosby presides over the decanting of the dinner wine. Not shown are daughters Erinn, Ensa and Evin.

PAUL ROBESON AND WIFE ESLANDE are met at Kennedy Airport upon their return to the United States at the completion of five-year world concert tour in January 1964. Son, Paul, Jr., wife and grandchildren, Susan and David, along with media, including EBONY editor Allan Morrison, make up the informal reception committee. Robeson's passport had been restored after controversy over Communist connections. Robeson responded to a question regarding his opinion of the Civil Rights Movement in the United States: "I have been a part of the Civil Rights Movement all of my life."

PAUL, JR. (L), PAUL ROBESON, SR. AND GRANDDAUGHTER, SUSAN (R.)

ALLAN MORRISON smiles with Paul Robeson.

Children with Disabilities-

Moneta Sleet. Jr.'s second son, Michael, is a victim of Down's Syndrome.

THIS is my son Mike. We had decided to do a story on the mentally retarded. Knowing that I had this personal feeling about mental retardation, I got this particular assignment. It was a labor of love. Really. It just happened that my son was in the school I covered. In this particular situation, he is taking some speech therapy from a wonderful lady who was his teacher. They were in the process of Mike learning to say the word 'Zip'. In the middle photograph Mike's hand is resting on his teacher's face, so that he can feel her pronouncing the word he is trying to say.

FOR those of you who have been exposed to the mentally retarded, you know that any small victory is a giant victory. In the course of these photographs, Mike is able to say the word 'Zip'. What is obvious is the feeling of elation and triumph that is reflected in both their faces.

Eleven-year-old Mike was one of an estimated five to six million mentally retarded children and adults in the United States in the year 1964 when this story was written and these photographs taken.

Date with a Dish

ALTHEA GIBSON won the women's singles title in the French Open Tennis Tournament on May 26, 1956. In 1957, she won both the Women's Singles championship at Forest Hills, N. Y., and at Wimbledon in England. Here she tosses salad and prepares for a light lunch with "Date with a Dish."

CARL ROWAN, former Ambassador to Finland and Director of the United States Information Agency, in 1964 with his wife, Vivien, prepares to eat the meal prepared for the EBONY food feature, "Date with a Dish."

JOHNNY MATHIS' career as a singer of love songs took off in the late 1950s with *Wonderful, Wonderful, Chances Are* and *It's Not for Me to Say*. His Patio Feast with Fish and Fowl was as big a hit with his guests as his singing and was the Date with a Dish in the July 1981 EBONY Magazine.

fashion -
Kids and Mom's

135

fashion - women

FASHIONS and photography that stand the test of time.

fashion - men

EBONY Magazine was in the forefront in utilizing male models and fashions.

WHEN YOU ARE DEALING WITH PEOPLE who really are renowned and are top stars or super stars,
they have a certain quality about them that makes you feel at ease.

Moneta Sleet, Jr.

THIS photograph of Billie Holiday, which was made while we were recreating some scenes from her autobiography, was made during a break in the session in a hotel room in Philadelphia, where she had been busted at one point for cocaine use. She just stopped and was relaxing and had her hand up to her face and was looking off. The robe she had on had dropped, and you could see all the track marks on her arms. It was a very pensive photograph, yet it was very sad.

THE WILL MASTIN TRIO WITH SAMMY DAVIS, JR. (l. to r.), Will Mastin, Sammy Davis, Jr. and Sam Sr., with musical arranger, Marty Stephens, appeared in Broadway musical with multitalented Davis. Will Mastin remained Davis' manager following his father's retirement for ill health. Sammy Davis, Jr. became a single starring act in night clubs, on stage and in film.

WONDERFUL *MR. WONDERFUL* was the EBONY cover story in December 1956. Sammy Davis, Jr. starred with Chita Rivera (r.) and Olga James (l.) in the show that opened at New York's Broadway Theatre on March 22, 1956, and ran for a year.

LENA HORNE opened October 31, 1957, at the Imperial Theatre on Broadway in *Jamaica*. Her co-stars were Ricardo Montalban, Adelaide Hall, Ossie Davis and Josephine Premice.

OPENING NIGHT CROWD

DR. RALPH BUNCHE arrives at theatre.

AFTER SHOW, Billy Strayhorn (c.) and Lena.

LENA and husband, Lenny Hayton, leave theatre.

sports legends

JACKIE ROBINSON is shown with Branch Rickey, his wife, Rachel Robinson, and his mother, Mallie, following his Hall of Fame Induction in Cooperstown, N.Y. in 1962.

HE *(Jackie Robinson) was one of my heroes, just like Joe Louis. He was symbolic, and he was so eloquent and such a fighter for what he believed in, for what he felt the position of Blacks in this country should be.*

MUHAMMAD ALI (Cassius Clay) works out on race track in Kentucky, 1963.

TENNIS STAR ARTHUR ASHE was the first Black American to win at Wimbledon by defeating champion Jimmy Conners and in the World Championship Tennis Singles by defeating Bjorn Borg. He was also the first Black American named to a Davis cup team, which he captained in 1981.

REGGIE JACKSON, Yankee Stadium–The baseball great in a pensive mood.

Josephine Baker Comes Back to New York

THE LEGENDARY JOSEPHINE BAKER, the expatriate entertainer, comes home.

IMAMU AMIRI BARAKA (LeRoi Jones), prize-winning play-wright and civil rights activist, 1969

ROMARE BEARDEN, artist, 1984. His visual images of city life, churches, jazz clubs, front stoops and people, were immortalized through the medium of collage.

IMAMU AMIRI BARAKA, 1996 Olympics in Atlanta, Ga.

WHITNEY HOUSTON, singer and actress, whose *I Will Always Love You* from motion picture *The Bodyguard* won numerous awards, including a Grammy, also starred in the film version of the novel *Waiting to Exhale*. The daughter of gospel star Cissy Houston, Whitney started her climb to stardom as a model.

ANDRE WATTS, a gifted pianist, started his career at the age of 9 when he was performing on the Philadelphia concert stage. The son of an Hungarian mother and an African-American G.I., Watts' young childhood was spent on numerous U.S. Army Posts in Europe and the United States. At the age of 17 he appeared with the New York Philharmonic under the direction of Leonard Bernstein. He has won numerous awards and regularly performs the symphonic concert schedules of the world's major orchestras as a guest artist.

CHARLES GORDONE won the 1970 Pulitzer Prize for *No Place to Be Somebody*. He was the first Black to win for Drama.

Black dramatists move to center stage with Pulitzer Prizes

CHARLES FULLER'S *A Soldier's Play* won the 1982 Pulitzer for Drama. He was the second Black to win. It became a hit film as *A Soldier's Story*.

NEGRO ENSEMBLE COMPANY cast for *A Soldier's Play*, directed by Douglas Turner Ward, included Denzel Washington, Adolph Caesar and Samuel L. Jackson. It received rave reviews when it opened in New York and won the New York Drama Critics Award and the Outer Critics and Theatre Club Awards.

honors and awards

WOLE SOYINKA OF NIGERIA, 1986
Nobel Laureate for Literature

METROPOLITAN OPERA STAR LEONTYNE PRICE,
1965 Spingarn Medalist, is with NAACP
Executive Director Roy Wilkins, Metropolitan
Opera's Rudolph Bing and Arthur Spingarn,
chairman of the Board, NAACP.

ARETHA FRANKLIN, singer, pianist and songwriter, brought the cadence of gospel to popular rhythm and blues with *R-E-S-P-E-C-T*.

WHOOPI GOLDBERG, actress and comedian, won the Golden Globe and NAACP Image Award for her role in *The Color Purple*.

PEARL BAILEY, singer whose dry wit and style were inimitable, won a 1967 Tony Award for starring role in *Hello Dolly* and served as Special Advisor to the U.S. Mission in the United Nations, 1975.

JAZZ TRUMPETER JOHN BIRKS "DIZZY" GILLESPIE in the pre-World War II years played in the bands of Cab Calloway and Earl "Fatha" Hines, where he worked with Charlie Parker. Later with Billy Eckstine, Gillespie formed a new group, which included Sarah Vaughn. Bebop was born. An arranger, composer and bandleader, Gillespie toured the world as State Department Ambassador in the "Cold War" period.

THEOLONIUS MONK started as a church organist and became one of the musicians credited with having changed the tempo of modern jazz. Winner of the 1959 Down Beat Critics poll, he set the pace as pianist and composer for young independent musicians who moved away from traditional jazz to "follow their own drummer."

MILES DAVIS, pace-setting jazz trumpeter and orchestra leader, created a subtle new form of "cool" jazz in response to the "Bebop" era.

COUNT BASIE with his great jazz band gave many singers and musicians their first major exposure.

STEVIE WONDER, multitalented child star, grew up to be just as awesome as an adult singer, pianist and composer. Winner of over 15 Grammy Awards, Wonder was inducted into the Rock and Roll Hall of Fame in 1989.

REDD FOXX was famous for his nightclub act and "adult " recordings long before he became a household name as Fred Sanford in the long-running TV series *Sanford and Son*.

The Many Faces of Lena

CLASSY AND SASSY was the title given to singer Sarah Vaughn in the early days of her career. Her voice was described by some critics as "divine" and her interpretation of lyrics as masterful. A contemporary of Billy Eckstine, Charlie Parker and Dizzy Gillespie, she was a jazz artist and a pioneer in her vocal style. She died in 1990.

DOROTHY DONEGAN, the famed jazz pianist photographed under sable, mink and chinchilla, was at the height of her career. Noted for her humor and sense of showmanship, Donegan travelled throughout Europe and the United States from the early 1940s when she first appeared in film and on Broadway. She was a recipient of the American Jazz Masters' Fellowship given by the National Endowment for the Arts in 1992. She died in Los Angeles on June 8, 1998.

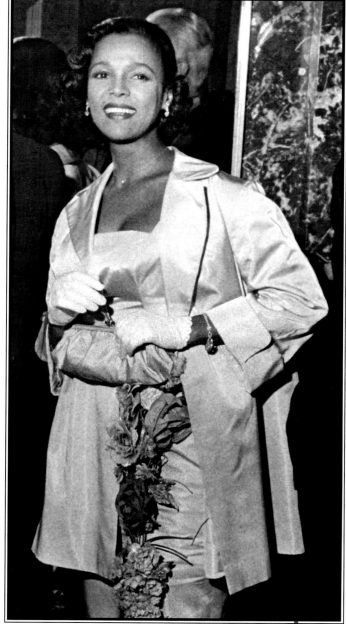

James Van der Zee, photographer, New York, 1970. Van der Zee, whose photographs of the Harlem of the 1920s and 1930s brought him fame during the last years of his life, died in 1983 at age 96.

Beautiful and tragic film star Dorothy Dandridge was the first African-American woman to be nominated for an Oscar as Best Actress for her role in *Carmen Jones*. She also starred in *Island in the Sun* and *Porgy and Bess*. She died in 1965.

establishment of Black Academy of Arts and Letters

SHIRLEY GRAHAM DUBOIS receives the First Hall of Fame citation for her late husband, Dr. W. E.B. DuBois, at the September 1970 Awards Banquet of the Black Academy of Arts and Letters (BAAL). The presentation was made by Dr. C. Eric Lincoln, president of BAAL. Prior to her husband's death, Mrs. DuBois lived with her husband in Ghana. Following the overthrow of Kwame Nkrumah, she made her home in Egypt and she was initially denied a visa to return to the United States for the Awards presentation. However, the Attorney General did grant a two-month visa, and Mrs. DuBois was present to accept the award. (G. Marshall Wilson photo)

C. JOHN HENRIK CLARKE presents the award to poet Mari Evans for her book, *I Am A Black Woman*.

KATHERINE DUNHAM, dancer and choreographer, receives award in 1971 for outstanding achievement in the arts.

A GROUP OF FIFTY BLACK SCHOLARS, authors, artists, educators and intellectuals gathered in Boston on March 27, 1969, to inaugurate the Black Academy of Arts and Letters (BAAL). Building on the foundation established in 1897 by the American Negro Academy led by Francis Grimke, Kelly Miller, W.E.B. DuBois and the aged Alexander Crummell, the group's mission was defined. It was dedicated to giving recognition to achievement by those engaged in cultural and intellectual pursuits. Dr. C. Eric Lincoln, author and professor of religion and sociology at Union Theological Seminary, was elected president. Other officers were novelist John O. Killens, vice president; editor and journalist Doris E. Saunders, secretary; and psychiatrist Dr. Alvin Poussaint, treasurer. Among the founding members were Inge Hardison, sculptor; Charles Hamilton, political scientist; Benjamin Quarles and Lerone Bennett Jr., historians; Charles White and Floyd Coleman, artists; Etta Moten Barnett, singer; Vertis Hayes, painter and sculptor; Dorothy Porter Wesley, librarian; Adelaide Cromwell Hill, Africanist scholar; and Margaret Walker Alexander, author and poet. Funded by a three-year grant from the Twentieth Century Fund, the group developed a critique for African-American scholars, held a major conference on the State of Black Arts and Letters and gave three major awards programs prior to its dissolution in 1974.

Black Academy Awards Excellence

AWARDEE MARI EVANS AND BILL COSBY, who acted as emcee for the evening, share a light moment with BAAL guest.

BAAL BOARD MEMBER AND TREASURER DR. ALVIN POUSSAINT, Singer Harry Belafonte and a friend enjoy Second Awards Banquet at New York's Waldorf Astoria Hotel.

NEW YORK PUBLIC LIBRARY'S Schomburg Library Curator Jean Blackwell Hutson receives the Hall of Fame citation from Dorothy Porter Wesley, librarian of Howard University's Moorland-Spingarn Collection.

AT THE EVENING'S END, Ruby Dee accepts the thanks of the Black Academy's President, Dr. C. Eric Lincoln, on behalf of the Academy and its guests for co-chairing the program and for a wonderful evening.

Bill Cosby and Sleet-The Cosby Show wrap

THE MAY 1992 issue of EBONY Magazine in Backstage, the editor's introduction to stories behind stories that are running in the magazine, depicts a group scene from the last taping of *The Cosby Show*. The scene which depicts son Theo Huxtable's graduation from college had a surprise actor playing the role of "Uncle Thornhill," who although crippled had come to see his nephew graduate. The man portraying" Uncle Thornhill," after formalities were cleared by the actor's union, was Moneta Sleet, Jr. Sleet, with EBONY senior editor Laura Randolph, was on the set to cover and photograph the taping of the last episode of the long-running (eight years) television show. When Bill Cosby decided that Sleet should be in the last episode of the show that made the Huxtable family a part of all of America, he was paying tribute to the admiration and respect that existed between the two men.

The phenomenal success of *The Cosby Show*, starring Bill Cosby as Dr. Cliff Huxtable and Phylicia Rashad as his wife, Claire, revolves around their children. They are a son and three daughters from early teen to young adult. They have an engaging four-year-old sister named Rudy, who worked her way into the hearts of the American viewing audience. The trials and tribulations of the upper middle-class Black family broke new ground on television and set new standards for excellence in family entertainment from its first airing in September 1984 until the last show. *The Cosby Show* was NBC's all-time ratings winner, crossing all demographic groups for audience share.

A 1985 PHOTOGRAPH OF THE HUXTABLE FAMILY, (clockwise, from top l.), Lisa Bonét as Denise (not with the show in the final year), Malcolm-Jamal Warner as Theo, Phylicia Rashad as Claire Huxtable, Dr. William (Bill) Cosby as Dr. Cliff Huxtable, Keshia Knight Pulliam as Rudy and Tempest Bledsoe as Vanessa.

PHYLICIA RASHAD (Claire Huxtable) understandingly helps Keshia Knight Pulliam (Rudy, who was a four-year-old at the beginning of the show and at the final episode was becoming a teenager) to cope with the problems of being the youngest of the siblings in the final shooting.

IN TOUCHING MOMENT, Malcolm-Jamal Warner as son Theo is passed the symbolic blue and red baton by Cosby. As his father, Dr. Cliff Huxtable, this moment following Theo's graduation from college provided the setting for the final episode of the phenomenally successful television situation comedy.

DR. WILLIAM COSBY consults with friend, Dr. Alvin Poussaint, the program's technical consultant and a Harvard University Medical school professor and psychiatrist. Poussaint's role was to monitor the scripts in order that the level of humor, warmth and balanced honesty be maintained.

THE ENTIRE CAST and crew of *The Cosby Show* and network executives assemble for a final photograph as Bill Cosby, the star and creative force behind the show, greets cast members and the studio audience.

Olympics, 1996

THE BID FOR THE CENTENNIAL OLYMPIC GAMES was won by Atlanta, and the United States was set to host the historic feat in 1996. Bringing the games to Atlanta had been accomplished by the work of former Atlanta Mayors Maynard Jackson and Andrew Young and the current mayor William "Bill" Campbell. This trio of bright and able African-American executives had executed a coup that would have been unthinkable a score of years earlier. An additional achievement was the election of Dr. LeRoy T. Walker, former chancellor of North Carolina Central University, to be president of the United States Olympic Committee. He was the first African-American to preside over this prestigious committee, a non-paid position. It was Atlanta's finest hour.

DR. LeRoy T. Walker

CYNTHIA JONES, president, Jones-Worley Design, consults with colleague on service to the large number of orders for displays and parades.

DURING OPENING CEREMONIES IN ATLANTA, the United States team follows the flag. Dr. LeRoy T. Walker, president of the United States Olympic Committee, holds hat aloft.

SHIRLEY FRANKLIN AND KAY WALLACE, two African-American women, play major role in Olympic planning as senior executives at the Atlanta Committee for the Olympic games.

THE COLORFUL FLAGS OF NIGERIA AND SOUTH AFRICA wave as the teams they represent are led in for the historic Olympic competition. It was the beginning of 16 days of games and only the second in which South African athletes had competed following the nation's banning in 1964 because of the apartheid system, which did not allow Black athletes to compete equally with Whites.

AT GAMES' END; competitions completed and winners declared, the Olympic Flag is lowered.

part three:
FAMILY ALBUM
COMPLETED

"I HAVE NEVER WANTED TO LIVE IN ANOTHER COUNTRY. This is home. I certainly was happy going to Africa. But, I am an American. There is a lot of work to be done here. Through my camera, it is this country and its people I hope to portray."

Moneta Sleet, Jr.

Moneta Sleet, Jr.,
Pulitzer Prize-Winning Photojournalist
New York Public Library
Fifth Avenue and 42nd Street
September 19–November 8, 1986

THIS EXHIBIT OF MONETA SLEET'S PHOTOGRAPHS was one of many over the two decades following the awarding of the Pulitzer Prize. It was particularly rewarding to Moneta Sleet, Jr., however, because it brought together his body of work before an audience of more than 600 friends, family, colleagues and community leaders. Jointly sponsored by Johnson Publishing Company, Inc. and the Philip Morris Company, Inc., it received warm reviews in the mainstream media as well as the Black press. Stanley Scott, vice president and director of Corporate Affairs for Philip Morris, said, "We are both proud and honored to be associated with an artist such as Moneta Sleet." John H. Johnson, editor and publisher, Johnson Publishing Company, Inc., described Sleet as a "highly motivated and dedicated individual. Marked by his grace, style and sincerity, his photographs have given us an important record of Black history for the last 30 years." Pictured above are (l. to r.) Valerie Wilson, Emmy Lou Wilson, Moneta Sleet, Jr., Gregory Sleet, Mary Grantham Sleet and Juanita Sleet.

SLEET JOINS JPC FAMILY: EBONY Senior Editor Lerone Bennett Jr., EBONY managing editor Hans Massaquoi, John H. Johnson, publisher, Johnson Publishing Company, Charles Sanders, EBONY managing editor, Lydia J. Davis, vice president-director of Promotions and Jeff Burns, New York Eastern Advertising director.

JOHN H. JOHNSON joins Geoffrey Holder, Moneta Sleet, Jr., George Weissman, former chairman & CEO of Philip Morris Companies, Inc. and Stanley Scott, **vice president** and Director of Public Affairs, Philip Morris Companies, Inc.

ARTHUR ASHE, WIFE, JEANNE, AND SLEET

Sleet with family

WITH SON GREGORY, Moneta Sleet, Jr. leaves en route to an overseas assignment.

AT HALLOWEEN PARTY in the home of Vice President Albert Gore in 1994, he is with wife, daughter Lisa, and three grandchildren, Moneta III, Ashlee and Kelsi.

HE EMBRACES his wife, Neet.

HE POSES WITH GRANDSON Moneta III in backyard at home.

Sleet with colleagues and friends

WITH LONG-TIME FRIEND and colleague G. Marshall Wilson, who was also a staff photographer at Johnson Publishing Company.

WITH LERONE BENNETT JR., who worked with Sleet on many assignments.

FIRST ANNUAL NATIONAL ASSOCIATION OF BLACK JOURNALISTS AWARDEES

AN AUTOGRAPHED photo from Mrs. Barbara Bush to Moneta Sleet, Jr.

SLEET IN OFFICIAL WHITE HOUSE PHOTO shoot. He photographs Mrs. Barbara Bush in White House living quarters.

EBONY STAFF PHOTOGRAPHERS–1972
G. Marshall Wilson, Isaac Sutton,
Moneta Sleet, Jr. and Maurice Sorrell

PULITZER PRIZE WINNERS honored by Honeywell in 1975.
(Monroe S. Frederick photo)

SLEET RECEIVES Overseas Press Club Award in 1958.
(G. Marshall Wilson photo)

URBAN LEAGUE AWARD–Percy Sutton makes presentation. Andrew
Hatcher is in background. (Gilbert Pictorial Enterprise photo)

SLEET WITH SONS OF MARTIN LUTHER KING, JR., Martin L. King, III and Dexter. (Maurice Sorrell photo)

TRIP TO SOUTH AFRICA on Gore Plane -May 1994. (official White House photo)

SLEET AND HIS BUDDIES, Jackie Robinson Jazz Concert–June 1979. (Richard Massey photo)

ON SAFARI with Era Bell Thompson in East Africa, 1969.

AT OPENING OF EXHIBIT of *Songs of My People*, with Gordon Parks, his long-time friend, and Howard Bingham, photographer. (Fred Watkins photo)

WITH YOUNG CHILDREN AROUND HIM in Timbuktu while on assignment, 1972.

Death and Funeral of

WHEN THE OLYMPIC FLAG WAS LOWERED and his film dispatched to Chicago for processing, Moneta Sleet, Jr. packed his cameras and returned to his wife and family in Baldwin, Long Island, for those precious last days before the journey "home." He died on Monday, September 30, 1996, at Columbia-Presbyterian Medical Center in New York City. He was just 70. Perhaps, ironically, Moneta's last professional assignment was covering the 1996 Olympic Games in Atlanta, Ga. Among other things, we think of the Olympics as the ultimate competition–a gathering of those of superior attainment, a gathering of Olympians. To any such meeting of those in his chosen profession, Sleet, as he was known to friends and colleagues, would certainly have been one of the first called. He was the winner of the first Pulitzer Prize for Feature Photography as well as a multitude of other awards and honors–he was, indeed, an Olympian.

Sleet was a master of his craft who left history a body of work that is extraordinary in its scope and quality. Yet, for all his professional accomplishments, those who knew him well know that of which he was most proud, that which gave him the most joy–his marriage of forty-six years to Juanita, and his legacies: his children, Gregory, Michael and Lisa, and his grandchildren, Moneta III, Ashlee and Kelsi.

Moneta Sleet, Jr.

THE REV. JOE ROWE, pastor, leads the call to celebrate the life of Moneta Sleet, Jr.

REV. NORMAN O. RATES, childhood friend, reads eulogy.

GREGORY M. SLEET, his eldest son, reads the 23rd Psalm.

celebration of the life of Moneta Sleet, Jr.– tributes and reflections

MICHAEL HARRIS, NEPHEW

LERONE BENNETT JR., executive editor, EBONY Magazine, and friend

BERTRAND D. MILES, photographer, colleague and friend

GORDON PARKS, Photographer, Mentor, Friend

JOHN H. JOHNSON, publisher, CEO, Johnson Publishing Company, Inc. and friend.

Our Father, Who Art in Heaven...

FAMILY makes way to chapel for last rites.

FLAG-FOLDING CEREMONY is held for World War II veteran at Calverton Cemetery.

JUANITA SLEET places rose in farewell to husband of forty-six years.

GRANDSON MONETA SLEET III pays tribute with rose.

How Great Thou Art...

His Eye is On the Sparrow...

173

Can I get a witness?

That's the question, especially for people who stand at a point in history with their backs against the wall.
For people on both sides of that wall, for high and low, Black and White, the central
question is:

Can I get somebody to confirm my reality?
Can I get somebody to say I was there?
Can I get somebody to tell my story and say Amen and Hallelujah?
Can I get a witness?

Moneta Sleet, Jr., my brother and teacher and friend, answered that
question with his eye and his soul and his life.

He came up from Owensboro, Kentucky, up from segregation, up from Jim Crow schools and buses and cameras, and in the
end by some miracle no one can explain he not only endured but prevailed, becoming one of the greatest photographers in
the Republic and leaving a collection of indelible images that will never die.

Sleet--everybody called him Sleet--was there.

He had a camera, and he saw it all:

Haile Selassie in his doomed glory, Kwame Nkrumah at the beginning of the African Revolution, Adam Clayton Powell and
Thurgood Marshall and Martin Luther King, Jr. at the beginning of the American Revolution, Rosa Parks on a Montgomery
bus, Aretha Franklin singing R-E-S-P-E-C-T.

Sleet was there.

He saw the sun rise in Harlem, marched in Selma and Washington, photographed the crucifixions and the resurrections in
Atlanta and Johannesburg.

I had the honor of working with him for forty-one years. We covered Sammy Davis Jr.'s first triumph on Broadway, Nat King
Cole's last TV show, Jomo Kenyatta in Kenya, Nelson Mandela in South Africa, Martin Luther King, Jr. at the beginning of his
journey in Montgomery and at the beginning and end in Atlanta. I played a small role in helping him get the photograph of
Coretta Scott King and her daughter, Bernice, at the King funeral. I agree with Publisher John H. Johnson who said that one of
the most fascinating aspects of that moment was that Sleet made the wrath of man praise him by becoming a witness for both
truth and excellence. For although some of the best photographers in the world were in that church, the photographer with
the keenest eye, the firmest grip and the softest touch was the photographer some people tried to exclude.

And here we come to the miracle of Moneta, for in the end the witness became the subject and the story-teller became the
story and the picture-taker became a picture and a promise and a truth.

During this period, and later, almost without anybody noticing, except his beloved "Neet," who told him that he was a
Pulitzer prize-winner before he won the Pulitzer Prize, Sleet became an institution. People started calling EBONY and asking
for him specifically. Sammy Davis, Jr. was blunt. "Send Sleet." Coretta Scott King and the King children and Maya Angelou
always asked, "Can Sleet come?" Bill Cosby said he was having an intimate sit-down dinner for his wedding anniversary
and that he didn't want press within a hundred miles, but that Sleet could come.

But we must not think, we dare not think, that he was a witness for the great alone. Many, perhaps most, of his best photographs are of the people, and I've always believed with him that one of his greatest photographs was the photograph of The
Woman on the Road To Montgomery.

What makes this photograph memorable is that most of the action is internal. Having overcome segregation, sorrow, hard
words and hard knocks, The Woman in the photograph is marching along behind King with her eyes closed, singing a
Freedom Song, clapping her hands, saying with her whole body, with her whole soul, not that she is on the way to the mountaintop, but that she is on the mountaintop, with the saints, looking over into the Promised Land.

Sleet saw all that because he saw not only with the eyes of the body but also with the eyes of the spirit. And the greatest tribute we can pay him and Juanita Harris Sleet, who climbed the mountain with him, is to open our eyes and our spirit to this
great collection of photographs and to see with him the tragedy, grandeur and triumph of fifty years that changed us forever.

LERONE BENNETT JR.
June 10, 1998

acknowledgements

IT IS IN THE CONTEXT OF MONETA SLEET, JR. as a working photographer on assignment that these photographs have been assembled. Sleet was the staff man doing his job, whenever and wherever that assignment took him. In his work, an assignment might range from shooting a fashion layout , a "Date with a Dish" spread or following a story to such exotic, far-off places as Surinam or Senegal, Moscow or Monrovia. For Sleet, it was essential that his passport be kept current. From 1955 to 1996, with his cameras he travelled for Johnson Publishing Company, Inc. and recorded with his special "eye" the unfolding of history.

In putting this volume together we had the encouragement and cooperation of Sleet's family, especially his devoted wife, Juanita, or "Neet" as she is called, and his eldest son, Gregory. They were particularly helpful in supplying family photographs, identifications, wording, the right nuances and encouragement throughout the months that we worked on the project.

Moneta Sleet, Jr.'s warm and close friend, Gordon Parks Sr., one of the twentieth century's pre-eminent creative artists, has written the introduction to this volume. We thank him for his immediate and warm response.

We also had the cooperation and good wishes of Sleet's long-time friend, the late Harvey Russell, who helped in identifying persons in photographs from the era of the fifties and sixties.

We are grateful for the work of colleagues, such as veteran Johnson Publishing Company photographer, the late G. Marshall Wilson, whose photographs of the Sleet family at the announcement of the Pulitzer Prize and on other occasions are used in this volume, and for the work of the late Maurice Sorrell, who worked closely with Sleet over the years.

Staff Photographer Monroe Frederick, II's photos of the New York Public Library Photographic Exhibition in 1986 give an indication of the appreciation of Moneta Sleet's work by the public and his peers. Vandell Cobb, staff photographer based in the Chicago office, was generous in offering technical knowledge and constructive criticism during the selection process.

Lloyd Redwing and Laurnetta A. Martin are meticulous craftspersons, and their skill in rescuing older negatives and prints for use in this volume was invaluable.

The Art Department's Cathy D. Reedy assisted in keeping the large number of photographs from becoming lost in confusion and chaos as they went through the various procedures required for printing in the new technologies.

The special library of Johnson Publishing Company is a treasure-trove of knowledge and information. Mrs. Pamela Cash Menzies, librarian, and library assistant Hope Rogers were forthcoming and helpful in assisting with documenting dates, quotations, spelling foreign names and places and ferreting out other obscure information.

JET Senior Editor Sylvia Flanagan was always responsive to our requests for assistance, and EBONY and JET Magazines' Copy Editor Phyllis R. Horton was meticulous in proofreading and correcting errors in voice, tense and redundancies.

Basil Phillips' stewardship of the photographic files of Johnson Publishing Company over the past several decades is legendary. He had the good fortune to work closely with Moneta Sleet, Jr. as he was organizing photo exhibits that travelled from New York to Atlanta and other places around the country. Without Basil Phillips' assistance and that of his assistant, Vickie Wilson, my task would have been incredibly more difficult.

Art Director Raymond A. Thomas has brought his talent and creativity to help produce this beautiful collection of Moneta Sleet, Jr.'s work. His jacket design projects the vision that Moneta Sleet's photography exemplifies in *Special Moments*.

The Book Division's Mrs. Lillian Terrell has provided a sympathetic and knowledgeable sounding board for me.

The opinions and resourcefulness, particularly on the New South Africa section, of Mrs. Linda Johnson Rice, president and COO, were greatly appreciated.

However, without the insight and sensitivity of Johnson Publishing Company's founder and CEO John H. Johnson, the resources that have been necessary for assembling this volume would neither exist nor be available for use at this time. It was his foresight that created the environment that permitted a cadre of brilliant photo-journalists to develop in the milieu of EBONY and JET Magazines. Moneta Sleet, Jr. was in the forefront of this group.

Finally, I am personally grateful to John H. Johnson for allowing me the privilege of compiling and editing this volume. I considered Moneta Sleet, Jr. a friend and colleague. I admired his talent as reflected in his work. I was in awe of his unfailing good nature and warm smile.

Any shortcomings in this volume, therefore, are mine. I accept the responsibility.

DORIS E. SAUNDERS
June 1, 1998

PHOTO CREDITS:

All photographs in this volume, unless expressly
acknowledged, are the work of Moneta Sleet, Jr.
To:
Mrs. Juanita Harris Sleet, who opened her family albums and
shared with us so that they might be shared with the reader.
To:
Staff photographers of Johnson Publishing Company,
G. Marshall Wilson and Maurice Sorrell, we express our appreciation.
To:
Monroe S. Frederick Photo
Gilbert Pictorial Enterprise
Official White House Photographers
To:
Beth McKenty and The Community Relations-Social
Development Commission, Milwaukee, Wisconsin, whose
publication *Faces of America, 1978* contained an interview
with Moneta Sleet from which we have extracted quotes.

The following videotaped interviews with
Moneta Sleet, Jr. were resources:

An interview with Moneta Sleet in *A Portrait of Two
Photographers*, Kentucky Educational Television Network, 1988

An Interview with Moneta Sleet, Kodak Business Television,
February 13, 1992

An Interview with Moneta Sleet, July 11, 1993, by St. Louis Art
Museum

Our Thanks.

Index

A

Abernathy, Rev. Ralph, 40
Abyssinia (see Ethiopia)
Ade, Sunny King, 79
Adjei, Ako, Minister of the
    Interior, Tunis, 56
Africa
    Nixon tour 43-57, 60-71
    (see also individual country)
    Sleet on, 42
    Africa and the World, 43-71,
        76-87
Africa and the United Nations,
    98-99
African National Congress
    (ANC), 84-87
Ahidjo, Ahmadou, President,
    Cameroons
    Young Mission to Africa, 76-79
Ahman, Matthew National
    Catholic Conference, 21
Akintola, Premier Chief Samuel L.
    Nigeria, 57
Ako Adjei, Tunisian
    Minister, Interior, 54
Al-Mahdi, Abdul Rahman, 52
Al-Mirghani, Ali, 52
Alabama
    Bus Boycott, 16-17
    Selma to Montgomery
    March, 31-33
    State Guard, Nationalized, 32
Alexander, Margaret Walker,
    156
Ali, Muhammad (Cassius
    Clay), 113, 140
Allen, Debbie, 115, 129
Allensworth, Ozetta,
    (see Sleet, Ozetta
        Allensworth)
Alpha Phi Alpha Fraternity, 9
American Negro Academy, 156
Americans for Democratic
    Action, 23
Amina, Lala Princess,
    Morocco, 43
Amsterdam News, 12
Anderson, Marion, 23, 116
Anderson, Reuben
    Mississippi Supreme Court,
        106
Andrews, Julie, 116

Angelou, Maya
    Clinton Inaugural, 124
    New South Africa, 74
Ansar Moslem, Sudan, 52
Anthony, Bank, 79
Apollo Theatre, N.Y., 18
Arap-Moi, Daniel, President,
    Kenya, 76-79
Arafat, Yasser, Chairman,
    Palestine Liberation
        Org. (PLO), 80, 87
Aronson, Arnold, 23
Arts Festival, First Negro World,
    64-67
Ashe, Arthur, 159,164
Ashe, Mrs. Arthur (Jeanne
    Moutousammy), 164
        daughter, Camera, 130
Associated Negro Press,
    (ANP), 43
Associated Press (AP)
    Sleet, pool photographer
        at King funeral, 36, 41
Astronauts, Black, 107
Atlanta (Ga.)
    Olympics, 1996, 160-161
    Students in Russia, 72-73
Atwater, Stanley, 72
Avant, Clarence
    Young Mission to Africa, 79
Ayers-Allen, Phylicia, (see
    Rashad, Phylicia)
Azikiwe,Nnamdi, 58-59
B
Babangida, Ibrahim Gen'l,
    Nigeria, 80
Bailey, Pearl, 123, 136, 150
Baker, Constance, (see
    Motley, Constance Baker)
Baker, James, U.S. Sec'y of State,
    80
Baker, Josephine, 22, 141
Balafrej, Ahmed, Foreign
    Minister, Morocco,43
Balewa, Sir Alhaji Abubakar
    Tafewa, Prime Minister,
        Nigeria, 58
Baldwin, James, 23, 140
Bankhead, Tallulah, 131
Baoule Tribe,
    Mask, 95
Baraka, (Imamu) Amiri,

    128, 146
Barnes, Nathan, U.N.
    Ambassador, Liberia, 62
Barnett, Claude
    Africa, 43, 55
    Ethiopia, 51
Barnett, Mrs. Claude
    (Etta Moten)
    Black Academy of Arts and
        Letters, 156
    Ethiopia, 50
    Morocco, 43
    Uganda, 48
Basie, William (Count), 152
Basilica (see Ivory Coast)
Bates, Daisy, 23
Bearden, Romare, 146
Beitel, Dan, 35
Bekkai, M'Barek, Premier
    Morocco, 43
Belafonte, Harry,
    Black Academy of Arts and
        Letters, 157-158
    March on Washington, 23
    Inaugural Gala, 116
    King Funeral, 38
Bello, Sir Alhaji Ahmadu, 58, 62,
Bennett, Lerone Jr.
    Afterword, 175
    Annual Black Achievement
        Awards, 115
    Black Academy of Arts and
        Letters, 156
    King Funeral, 36
    New South Africa, 84
    Sleet and Bennett, 166
    Sleet Funeral, 172
    What Manner of Man, biog of
        Dr. Martin Luther
            King, Jr., 26
Bethune, Mary McLeod, 21
Bevel, Rev. James 33
Bey of Tunis, Sidi Mohammed
    al Amin, 54
"Big Red" (see Orange, Rev.
    James), 32,
Binaisa, Godfrey, President,
    Uganda, 76-78
Bing, Rudolph, 149
Black Academy of Arts and
    Letters (BAAL), 156-157
Black Committee Awards,

50th American Presidential
    Inaugural, 122
Black Republican Council of 100,
    123
Blake, Rev. Eugene Carson, 21
Bluford, Lt. Col. Guion S., 105
Booker, Juanita, 120
Booker, Simeon
    Annual Black Achievement
        Awards, 115
    Ethiopia, 51
    Nixon African Tour, 43
Botsio, Komo (Ghana), 44
Bourguiba,Habib, Premier
    Tunis, 56
Bradley, Tom, Mayor
    Los Angeles (Calif.), 114
Brathwaite-Burke, Yvonne, Rep.
    (D-Calif.), 100
Braun, Carol Moseley, Sen. (D-
    Ill.), 86, 107, 115
Brooke, Edward W., Sen. (R-
    Mass.), 91
Brooks, Angie, President U.N.
    General Assembly, 98-99
(see also United Nations)
Brotherhood of Sleeping Car
    Porters, 21
Brown, Jim, 111
Brown, Michael Arrington, 108
Brown, Mrs. Oscar Brown, Jr.
    (Maxine), 116
Brown, Oscar, Jr., 116
Brown, R(ichard) Jess, 34
Brown, Robert, 122
Brown, Ronald H.,
    Death, 108
    Democratic National
        Committee, 108
    Family, 108
    New South Africa, 84, 86
    Sec. of Commerce, U.S., 108
Brown, Mrs. Ronald H. (Alma
    Arrington), 108
Brown, Theodore (Ted), 21
Brown, Tracey Lyn, 108
Brown, Virginia Inness, 67
Bourguiba, Habib, President,
    Tunisia
    Nixon Tour, 56
Bunche, Ralph (Dr.),
    Inaugural, 1965, 117

March on Washington, 23
Opening Night, 143
United Nations, 97
Burton, Philip, Rep. (D-Calif.), 25
Bus Boycott
Montgomery, AL 16-17
Bush, Mrs. George (Barbara)
120, 166
Bush, George, H. W.
President, 122
Vice President, 120, 122
C
Caesar, Adolph, 148
Calhoun, Anna, 72
Calloway, Cabell (Cab), 113
Calloway, Mrs. Cab (Nuffie), 113
Campbell, William (Bill)
Mayor, Atlanta, Ga., 160
Cameroons
Young Mission to Africa,
68-69
Carmichael, Stokely, 25
Carter, Amy, 118
Carter, James Earl (Jimmy),
President, United States, 118-119
Carter, Mrs. Jimmy, (Rosalynn),
118
Caruthers, Paula, 72
Catholic Church, North
American College,55
Rome, 54-55
Chavis, Ben, 86
Cheek, Dr. James, 122
Cheyney, James, 25
Children, Disabilities, 133
Children's Defense Fund, 34-35,
Chisholm, Shirley, Rep.,
(D-N.Y.), 100
Christie, Cornell L.
Liberia, 60
Christian, Elizabeth, 72
Citizens Exchange Corp., 66
Civil Rights Commission ,14,16
Civil Rights Movement,16,106
(see also individual names)
Clarke, John Henrik,
Black Academy of Arts and
Letters, 156
Clarksdale, Mississippi, 106
(see also Mississippi)
Clay, Cassius
(see Ali, Muhammad)
Clay, William (Bill), Rep.,
(D-Mo.), 86
Clements, Rev. George H., 114
Clinton, Chelsea, 124
Clinton, William

Jefferson, President, U.S.
Inaugural, 1993, 124
Clinton, Mrs. William Jefferson,
(Hillary Rodham)
Inaugural, 124
New South Africa, 84-87
Cohn, Martin N., 35
Cole, Nat (King), 131
Cole, Natalie, 131
Cole, Dr. Johnnetta, 124
Coleman, Floyd, 156
Coliseum
Rome, 52
Congress of Racial Equality
(C.O.R.E.), 24
Connecticut, Hartford, 101
Conyers, John, Rep. (D-Mich.)
New South Africa, 86
Cook, Mercer, U.S.
Ambassador, Senegal
First World Festival of
Negro Arts, 66-69
Cook, Mrs. Mercer (Vashti
Smith), 66, 69
Cooks, Stoney, 40
Cooper, Russell, 18
Corbett, Willis W., 65
Cosby, Mrs. William (Camille
Hanks), 131
Cosby, Ennis W., 131
Cosby, Erinn, 131
Cosby, Ensa, 131
Cosby, Erika, 131
Cosby, Evin, 131
Cosby, Dr. William (Bill)
Black Academy of Arts and
Letters, 157
Cosby Show Wrap 157,158-
159
Family, 131
Council of Federated
Org. (COFO), 24-25, 35
Crawford, Sir Frederick, 48
Crummell, Alexander, 156
D
Dakar, Senegal
First World Festival of the
Arts, 62-63
Dandridge, Dorothy, 155
Daniels, Dwayne O.
Young Mission to Africa, 79
Date with a Dish ,134
Davis, Bella, 72
Davis, Miles, 151
Davis, Ossie, 156-157
Davis, Sammy Jr.
EBONY's 20th Birthday, 111

King Funeral, 38
March on Washington, 22
Mr. Wonderful, 142
Reagan Inaugural, 121
(see also Will Mastin Trio)
Dawson, William L., Rep.,
(D-Ill.), 90
Day of Prayer, National
Deliverance, 18-19
(see also Powell, Adam
Clayton, Jr.)
Dee, Ruby, 156-157
deKlerk, Frederick (F.W.),
President, Republic of
South Africa,
Namibia, 80
DeLavallade, Carmen, (Mrs.
Geoffrey Holder), 127
Dellums, Ronald V., Rep.,
(D-Calif.)
New South Africa, 84
Delzio, Frank
Young Mission to Africa, 79
Democratic Convention, 1964, 24
Desta, Ruth, Princess, Ethiopia, 97
Dexter Avenue Baptist Church
Montgomery, Ala., 17
Dickerson, Earl B., Mr. and Mrs.
1969 Inaugural, 117
Dinkins, David, Mayor, N.Y.
New South Africa, 84, 107
Disabilities, Children with, 133
Dixon, Julian, Rep., (D-Calif.), 87
Dixon, Sharon Pratt Kelly,
(see Kelly, Sharon)
Donegan, Dorothy, 154
Douglas, Helen Gahagan, 60
Down's Syndrome
(see Mental Retardation)
DuBois, Mrs. William E.B.
(Shirley Graham), 156
DuBois, William E.B.,
Nigeria, 58
Posthumous Award,
BAAL, 156
Dudley, Edward, 97
Duke, Angier Biddle, (Mrs.), 97
Dukes, Ofield
Young Mission to Africa, 79
Dunham, Katherine, 156
Dutton, Charles , 115
E
EBONY Magazine,
American Black Achieve-
ment Awards, 114-115
20th Anniversary, 111-113
50th Anniversary, 115

Edelman, Marian Wright, 35
(see Wright, Marian)
Eisenhower, Dwight, D.,
President, 43, 89
Eisenhower, Mrs. Julie Nixon, 117
Ellington, Edward K. (Duke)
First World Festival of the
Arts (Senegal), 66-68
Espy, Mike, Secretary,
Agriculture, U.S.
New South Africa, 84-87
Ethiopia (Abyssinia)
Nixon Tour, 49
Evans, Mari, 156-157
F
Fair Employment Practices
Commission, 21
Fakhoury, Pierre, 82
Families, 127-133
Family Album, 3-14 ,163-169
Family Importance
Sleet on, 126
Fashion, 135-139
Kids and Moms, 135
Male Models, 138-139
Women, 136-137
Firestone, Raymond
Liberia, 60
Fitzgerald, Ella, 114
Flanagan, Sylvia, 115
Fofana, Mrs. Binta Kinte, 64
Food
Date with a Dish, 134
Foxx, Redd, 152
Franklin, Aretha, 150
Franklin, Aretha, 150
Franklin, Janice, 72
Franklin, Shirley, 160
Freedom Summer (Mississippi),
24-25
(see also COFO (Council of
Federated Organizations))
Fresco, Paolo
Young Mission to Africa, 79
Fuller, Charles, 148
G
Gallagher, Francis, 55
Gambia, Juffre, 64
(see also Haley, Alex)
Gandhi, Mohandes K.
(called Mahatma Gandhi),
M. L. King as follower, 17
Ghana (formerly Gold Coast)
see also Nkrumah, Kwame
Independence 1957, 44-45
United Nations, 98-99
Gibson, Althea,

Date with a Dish, 134
Gillespie, Dizzy (John Birks
    Gillespie), 38, 80, 115, 151
Gilmer, Glenda, 72
King Funeral, 38
Gold Coast
    (see Ghana)
Goldberg, Whoopi, 150
Goodman, Andrew, 25
Gordone, Charles, 148
Gore, Albert Jr., Vice
    President, U.S.,
    New South Africa, 84-87
    Gore, Mrs. Albert (Tipper)
    New South Africa, 84-87, 168
Granger, Lester, 90
Granton, Fannie, 104
Gravely, Lt. Com. Samuel L., 103
Gray, William, Rep.(D-Pa.), 86
Great Britain
    Colonies gain
    Independence
    (see individual countries)
Green, Ernest,
    Clinton Inaugural, 125
New South Africa, 86
Greenwich Village (N.Y.)
    American Black Achieve-
        ment Awards, 114-115
Grimke, Francis, 156
Gregory, Dick
    American Black Achieve-
        ment Awards, 114
    Family, 128
    March on Washington, 23
Gronchi, Giovanni, 53
Guido, Paolo,
    Young Mission to Africa, 79
Guild of the Good Shepherd,
    Accra, Ghana, 45

H
Haddon, Thomas
    North American College in
        Rome, 55
Haiti, Representative at United
    Nations, 98
Haley, Alex
    Juffre, Gambia, 68-69
    Roots, 68
Haley, George, 68-69
Haley, Julius, 68-69
Halim, Mustafa
    Libyan Premier, 52
Hall of Fame, Cooperstown,
    N.Y., 140
Hall, Atty. Carsie
    Mississippi Freedom

Summer Cases, 34
Hamilton, Dr. Charles, 156
Hampton, Lionel
    Inaugurals, 117, 121, 123
Hardison, Inge, 156
Harris, Juanita
    (see Sleet, Mrs. Moneta)
Harris, Michael, 172
Hastie, Mrs. William (Beryl), 92
Hastie, William, Judge, 89, 92
Hatcher, Andrew, 167
Hawkins, Rep. Augustus F.
    (D-Calif.), 25
Hayes, Vertis, 156
Hayton, Lenny, 143
Height, Dorothy, 125
Henry, Aaron, 106
Herman, Alexis, 86, 124
Herrero Women
    Namibia, 81
Hill, Adelaide Cromwell, 156
Holder, Mrs. Geoffrey, 129
Holder, Geoffrey, 129
Holder, Leo, 129
Holiday, Billie, 141
Holman, M. Carl, 119
Holmes, Larry, 114
    Hooks, Benjamin
    FCC Commissioner, 103, 104
Horne, Lena
    Opening Night, 143
    Many Faces of Lena, 153
    March on Washington, 23
    EBONY, 20th Anniversary,
        111-112
Houphouët-Boigny, Felix
    Ivory Coast Basilica, 82-83
    United States, 94-95
Houphouët-Boigny, Mme. Felix,
    82-83, 94-95
Houston, Whitney, 147
Hudson, Dovie, 35
Hudson, Winston, 35
Hughes, Langston
    First World Festival of the
        Arts, 66-67
Humphrey, Dr. Hubert C., 65
Humphrey, Hubert H., Vice
President, U.S.
    Inaugural, 116
    King Funeral, 38
Humphrey, Mrs. Hubert H.
    Inaugural, 116
Hutson, Jean Blackwell, 157

I
Idris I., King of Libya, 52

Inaugurals,
    1965, 116
    1969, 117
    1981, 120
    1985, 121
    50th American Presidential
        Inaugural Black Committee
        Awards, 122
Irby, Ray, 119
Italy
    Nixon Tour, 53
Ivory Coast
    Basilica, 82-83

J
Jackson, Rev. Jesse
    Namibia Independence, 81
    New South Africa, 84-87
Jackson, Mahalia, 23
Jackson, Maynard
    Mayor, Atlanta, 118
    Olympics, 160
Jackson, Reggie, 144
James, Rt. Rev. Frederick, 84, 86
James, Olga, 142
Jawara, Dawda K, President,
    Gambia, 64
Jeffries, Leroy, 113
Jemison, Mae, 115
    (see also Astronauts)
Jeter, George Jr., 72
Johnson, Mrs. John H. Johnson
(Eunice Walker)
    Africa (Nixon Tour), 43-55
    Annual Black Achievement
        Awards, 114-115
    20th Anniversary,
        EBONY, 111-113
    Inaugurals, 117, 119, 120, 125
Johnson, Freddie, 72
Johnson, John H.,
    Publisher, CEO,
    Johnson Publishing Co., Inc
    Africa (Nixon Tour) 43-55
    Annual Black Achievement
        Awards, 114-115
    50th American Presidential
        Inaugural Black
        Committee Awards, 122
    Inaugurals, 117, 119, 120, 125
    Kenya Independence,
        Special Ambassador, 59
    King Funeral, 38
    Sleet Exhibit Opening, 163
    Sleet Funeral, 172
    20th Anniversary, EBONY,
        111-113
Johnson, Gen. Julius, 123

Johnson, Kaaren P., 122
Johnson, Linda, 120
    (see also Rice, Linda
        Johnson)
Johnson, Lyndon Baines,
    President, U.S., 32, 116
    Gift to Kenya, 59
Johnson, Robert E., Editor, JET
    Magazine
    Annual Black Achievement
        Awards, 115
    King Funeral, 36
    Young Mission to Africa, 76-79
Jones, Cynthia, 160
Jones, Le Roi
    (see Baraka, Amiri)
Jones, Quincy
    New South Africa, 84-87
Jones, Richard, American
    Ambassador to Liberia
    Nixon tour, 47
Jones, William
    American Consul to
        Liberia, 60
Jones-Worley Design Co., 160
Jordan, Barbara,
    U.S. Rep. (D-Texas), 100
Jordan, Vernon,
    Clinton-Gore Inaugural, 124
    National Urban League, 103
    New South Africa, 86

K
Khalil, Abdullah,
    Premier, Sudan, 50
Kasavubu, Joseph, President,
    Congo, 60
Kaunda, Kenneth, President,
Zambia
    Namibian Independence, 80
Kelly, Sharon Pratt, Mayor,
    Washington, D.C., 101
Kennedy, Edward Sen., (D-
Mass.), 38
Kennedy, Jacqueline (Mrs. John
    F.), 38, 94-95
Kennedy, John Fitzgerald,
    President, U.S.
    Houphouët-Boignys, 94-95
    Candidate, 90
Kennedy, Robert, Atty Gen'l,
    U.S., 95
Kennedy, Mrs. Robert, 95
Kent, Marina, Duchess of (Great
    Britain), 46
Kentucky, Owensboro
    birthplace, Sleet, M., 4-5
Kenya

Independence, 58
Kenyatta, Jomo, 58
Keys, Birdie Mae, 34
Khalil, Abdullah
    Premier, Sudan, 50
Khartoum, Sudan
    Steps (photo), 51
Kheel, Theodore W., 21
Killens, John O., 156
King, Mrs. Martin Luther, Sr.
(Alberta, mother), 39
King, Bernice, daughter, 37, 127
King, Dexter, son, 38, 127, 168
King, Mrs. Martin Luther King,
    Jr. (Coretta Scott),
        17, 37, 38, 40, 46, 86, 127
King, Rev. Martin Luther, Jr.
    Biography, *What Manner of
    Man*, 26
    Death and Funeral, 36-39
    Dexter Avenue Baptist
        Church, 17
    Family, 17, 36-39
    Ghana Independence, 46
    Ghandi, influence of,16
    March on Washington, 21-22
    Montgomery Bus Boycott, 16
    Nobel Peace Prize, 26-29,
    Selma to Montgomery, 31-32
King, Rev. Martin Luther, Sr.,
    39, 119
King, Martin Luther, III, son
    39, 127, 168
King, Yolanda, daughter, 17, 38
Kitchen, Robert
    Young Mission to Africa, 78
Kitt, Eartha
    King Funeral, 38
    daughter, Kitt, 129
Knight, Gladys, and the Pips, 114
Kremlin, 73
L
La Belle, Patti, 128
    son, Zuri
Lafontant, Jewel, Atty., 121
Lanning, Herman, Danish
    Ambassador to UN, 99
Larsson, Clotye Murdoch, 106
Lautier, Louis, 43, 55
Leadership Conference on Civil
    Rights, 23
Lewis, Ed
    New South Africa, 86
Lewis, John, Rep., (D-Ga.), 21-
    22, 25
    New South Africa, 84-87, 107
Lewis, Mrs. Minnie, 35

Liberia
    Nixon tour, 52
    Tubman Fifth Inaugural, 62-63
Libya, Tripoli
    Nixon Tour, 52
Lincoln, Dr. C. Eric,156-157
Llewellyn, Bruce,
    Young Mission to Africa, 76-79
Los Angeles, Calif.
    Muslim Mosque, 20
    Watts Riot (1963)
Lowery, Rev. Joseph E., 40
Lyman, Princeton Ambassador
to South Africa, U.S., p. 84-87
M
McAleese, Donald, 99
McDonald, Kitt, 129
Macharia, G.N.,
    game warden, 65
McHenry, Donald, 79
McKissack, Floyd
    Congress of Racial Equality
        (CORE), 21
McNair, Dr. Ronald, 105
McRae, Carmen, 115
McRee, Rev. James, 35
Magaldi, Philip, 55
Mahgoub, Ahmed, Foreign
    Minister, Sudan, 50
Mahoney, Charles, 92
Makeba, Miriam, 97
Malcolm X, 20
    (see also Shabazz, Malcolm)
Mali
    Federation of, 62
Malraux, André, 67
Mancharia, G. N., 70, 71
Mandela, Nelson, President,
    South Africa
    Clinton-Gore Inaugural, 125
    Namibian Independence, 80
    New South Africa, 84-87
Mandela, Mrs. Nelson
    (Winnie Nomzamo)
    Namibian Independence, 80
    New South Africa, 84
Mandinka Tribe,
    Gambia, 64
March
    on Washington, 21-23,
    Selma to Montgomery, 31
Margai, Sir Milton,
    Sierra Leone, 60
Marsalis, Wynton, 125
Marshall, Mrs. Norma, mother, 92
Marshall, Mrs. Thurgood
(Cecelia Suyat), 92

Marshall, Thurgood
    King Funeral, 38
    Marriage, 92
    NAACP, Special Counsel, 92
    Solicitor General, U.S., 112
    Supreme Court, U.S., 93
    20th Anniversary, EBONY, 111
Martin, Louis, 76-79
Martino, Gaetano, 53
Maryland State College-
    Princess Anne, 9
Massaquoi, Hans, 114-115, 164
Mastin, Will Trio, 142
    (see also Sammy Davis, Jr.)
Mathis, Johnny,
    Date with a Dish, 134
Mau Mau (Kenya), 58
Mbeki, Thabo,
    New South Africa, 85
Mboya, Tom, 59
Mental Retardation, 133
Meredith, Mrs. James,
    twin sons, James and
        Joseph, 126
Mercer, Mabel, 111
Mfume, Kweisi, Rep., (D-Md.)
New South Africa, 84-87
Miles, Bertrand D., 172
Miller, Kelly, 156
Mississippi Freedom Summer
    Project, 24-25, 35
Mitchell, Clarence, 23
    NAACP, Washington
        Bureau
Mohammed, V, Sultan,
    Morocco, 43
Mondale, Walter,
    Vice President, U.S.,
        Inaugural, 118, 119
Monk, Thelonious, 151
Montgomery, Ala.
    Bus Boycott , 16, 17
    March from Selma, 31
    Montgomery Improvement
        Ass'n, 18
Moore, Thomas, Jr.
    Young Mission to Africa, 77
Morocco
    Nixon tour, 43
Morrison, Allan, 132
Morrow, E. Frederick
    Nixon Tour, Africa, 43-55
    Special Ass't to President
        Eisenhower, 55
Moscow, Russia
    Atlanta Students Tour, 72-73
Moses, Robert, 24-25, 35

Moten, Etta
    (see Barnett, Etta Moten)
Motley, Constance Baker,
    Judge, 100
Murdock, Clotye,
    see Larsson, Clotye M.
Muslim Mosque, Los
    Angeles, Calif., 20
Mutesa II, Kabaka, Uganda, 48
N
Nabrit, Dr. James M., 113
Nairobi, Kenya, 60-61
Namibian Independence, 80-81
National Aeronautics and
    Space Administration,
        (NASA),105
National Association for the
    Advancement of Colored
        People (NAACP), 21-
            22, 34-35
National Association of Black
    Journalists (NABJ) Award, 166
National Catholic Conference
    for Interracial Justice, 21
National Council of Churches, 23
National Urban League, 90,
    Award to Sleet, 173
Negritude
    (see Senghor, Leopold)
Negro Ensemble Company, 148
Nicol, Davidson, 62
Nigeria
    Independence, 56
Nipson, Herbert, 114
Nixon, Rev. E. D.
    Montgomery Bus Boycott, 19
Nixon, Richard, President, U.S.
    1969 Inaugural, 117
    1973 Inaugural,117
    V.P., African tour, 43-55
        Rome, Italy, 53
Nixon, Mrs. Richard (Patricia)
    African Tour, 43-55
    1973 Nixon Inaugural,117
Nkrumah, Kwame, Prime
    Minister, Ghana
    Independence Ceremony,
        43-45

Nobel Prize, Literature (1986), 149
Nobel Prize, Peace (1964), 26-29
    Norway Oslo, Nobel Peace
        Prize ceremonies, 27-29
Nujoma, Sam, President
    Namibia, 80-81
Nyerere, Julius, President,
    Tanzania

Young Mission to Africa, 76

O

Obasanjo, Olusegun, President,
    Nigeria
        Young Mission to Africa, 76-79
Odiashvilly, Lena, 73
Odinga, A. Oginha, Kenya, 61
O'Neal, Frederick, 62
Orange, Rev. James, 33
Our Lady of Peace, Basilica,
    82-83
Our World Magazine, 11-13
Overseas Press Club Award, 167

P

Parham, Katherine, 18
Parks, Gordon, Sr.
    Introduction, VII
    125, 169, 172
Parks, Rosa, 16
Payne, Ethel L.
    Ethiopia, 51
    Nixon Tour, 43
    20th Anniversary,
        EBONY, 113
    Uganda, 48
Perez de Cuellar, Javier, U.N.
    Secretary-General
        Namibian Independence, 80
Pereira, Aristedes,
    Young Mission to Africa,
    76-79
Perry, Carrie Saxon, Mayor,
    Hartford, Conn., 101
Photography-School of Modern
    (N.Y.); 9
Pierce, Ponchitta, 116
Pierce, Samuel, 120
Pitt, Dr. David, 35
Plinton, Jimmy,
    TWA, East African Safari, 65
Poitier, Sidney,
    King Funeral, 38
Pool, Dr. Rosey, 62
Poor People's Campaign, 40
Pope-Roman Catholic Church
    John Paul II
        Ivory Coast Basilica,
            consecrated, 82-83
    Pius XII
        Nixon Tour, 53
Popkin, Ann, 25
Porters, Brotherhood of
    Sleeping Car, 21-22
Portrait of a Friend, VII
Potter, Rev. Dan M., 19
Poussaint, Alvin, Dr.
    Black Academy of Arts and

Letters, 156
The Cosby Show, 159
Powell, Rev. Adam Clayton, Jr.
    Rep.,U.S., (D-N.Y.)
    Day of Prayer, National
        Deliverance, 18-19
    Ghana Independence, 46
    House Com. Educ. and
        Labor, Chrm., 90
Powell, Colin , General,
    Chrm., Joint Chiefs of Staff
    New South Africa, 74-75
    U.S. Armed Forces, 109
Price, Leontyne, 149
Prinz, Joachim, Rabbi
    American Jewish Congress, 21
Protestant Council of N.Y., 19
Pulitzer Prize
    Sleet's reaction, 41
Pushkin, Alexander, 72-73

Q

Quaison-Sackey, Alex,
    African Nations at UN, 98-99
Quarles, Dr. Benjamin, 156

R

Racism
    Army, 8
Rahman Al-Mahdi, Abdul, 50
Randolph, A(sa) Philip
    Brotherhood of Sleeping
        Car Porters, 21-22
Rangel, Charles, Rep., (D-N.Y.)
    New South Africa, 74-75
Rashad, Phylicia, 127, 158-159
Rates, Rev. Norman O.
    Sleet Funeral, 171
Rauh, Joseph, 23
Reagan, Ronald, President, U.S.
    First Inaugural, 120
    Second Inaugural, 121
Reeves, Frank, 90
Resurrection City, 40
Reuther, Walter, President,
    AFL-CIO, 21
Rice, Linda Johnson
    American Black Achieve
        ment Awards, 115
    Inaugurals, 120, 125
    New South Africa, 84, 86, 87
Rickey, Branch, 144
Rivera, Alex, 48, 57
Rivera, Chita, 142
Roberson, James, Gov. Gen'l, 58
Roberts, Col. and Mrs.
    William A., 117
Robeson, David, 132
Robeson, Paul, 132

Robeson, Paul, Jr., 132
Robeson, Susan, 132
Robinson, David, 23
Robinson, Jackie
    Hall of Fame ,144
    Jazz Concert, 168
    March on Washington, 23
Robinson, Rachel, 144
Rockefeller, David,
    Liberia, 60
Rogers, John Jr., 121
Roman Catholic Priesthood
    North American College, 53
Rooney, Ellen, 72
Roosevelt, Franklin D.,
    President, U.S., 22
Roots
    (see Haley, Alex)
Rowan, Carl, 104, 134, 146
Rowe, Rev. Joe
    Sleet Funeral, 171
Rusk, Dean, Sec. of State, U.S., 116
Rusk, Mrs. Dean, 116
Rustin, Bayard
    March on Washington, 21-23
Ruth, Rev. Thurman, 18
Ryan, William F., Rep., (D-N.Y.), 25

S

Saint Petersburg, Russia, 72-73
Sanders, Charles, 27-29, 114
Sands, Diana, 111
Satcher, Dr. David, Surgeon
    General, U.S., 104
Saunders, Doris Evans
    Black Academy of Arts and
        Letters, 156
    Acknowledgements, 177
Schuyler, George, 113
Schwerner, Michael, 25
Scott, Hazel, 113
Segni, Antonio, Italian Premier, 53
Selassie, Emperor Haile
    Ethiopia, 49
    First World Festival of the
        Arts, 62
    U.N., New York, N.Y., 97
Senegal, 64-67
Senghor, Leopold
    President, Senegal, 64-67
    Young Mission to Africa,
        76-79
Shabazz, Betty (Mrs. Malcolm X)
    Family, 128
    Malcolm X Funeral, 30
    Namibian Independence, 80
Shabazz, Malcolm X
    Activities, 20

    Assassination, 30
    Los Angeles Mosque Police
        Raid, 20
Shagari, Alhaji Shehu,
    Young Mission to Africa, 76-79
Shevardnadze, Eduard A., 80
Shockley, Brenda, 72
Shuttlesworth, Rev. Fred J., 23
Simmons, Clifford, 62
Simms, Hilda, 112
Sleet, Gregory, 12, 40, 163, 171
Sleet, Mrs. Moneta Sleet, Jr.
    (Juanita), 9, 40, 163
Sleet, Lisa, 40, 163
Sleet, Michael, 40, 133
Sleet, Moneta J., Jr.
    birth, 4
    Black press
    camera, first, 7
    early life, 5, 6
    education, 7, 9
    Exhibit, New York Public
        Library, 163
    family, 40
    funeral, 171-173
    marriage, 11
    teaching, 9
    military service, 8
    movement, participant in, 16
    Olympics, 1996, 160
    parents
        educators, 7
    Moneta J., Sr., father, 4, 6
    Ozetta, mother, 4
    Emmy Lou (Wilson),
        sister, 5, 163
    photography as career, 9
    Pulitzer Prize, 41
    Safari, East Africa, 169
    Timbuktu, 169
Smythe, Mabel M. Ambassador,
    U.S., Cameroons
    Young Mission to Africa,
        76-79
Soldiers Play, 148
Songs of My People, Exhibit, 169
Sorrell, Maurice, 167
South Africa, Republic of,
    New South Africa, 84-87
South-West Africa People's
    Organization (SWAPO)
    Namibian Independence,
        80-81
Spingarn, Arthur, 149
Stokes, Louis, Rep., (D-Ohio)
    New South Africa, 74-75
Stokes, Ronald T.

Murder, 20
Stone, W. Clement, 120
Strayhorn, Billy, 143
Southern Christian Leadership
        Conference (SCLC), 21,24
Soyinka, Wole, 149
Student Non-violent
        Coordinating Comm.
                (SNCC), 21-22, 25
Sudan, Khartoum
        Nixon Tour, 50
Surinam Sunset, 75
Sutton, Isaac, 167
Sutton, Percy, 167
Sweden, Stockholm
        Nobel Prize trip, 27

T
Talbert, Hamilton, 120
Tanzania, East Africa
        Safari, 65
Temple, Herbert, 115
Thompson, Era Bell
        Safari in East Africa, 65
Till, Emmett,
        Murder, 106
Tobago Beach, 74
Tolbert, Sandra, 72
Tolbert, Stephen
        Liberia, 60
Tolbert, William R.
        President of Liberia, 60
        Vice President, 47, 60
        Young Mission to Africa, 76
Toote, Dr. Gloria E. A., 122

Trent, William, 113
Tsarskoye Selo, Russia, 72
Tubman, William V.S.
        President of Liberia, 47
        Inaugural (Fifth), 60-61
        Nixon Tour, 46
Tunis
        Independence, 56
Turner, W. Earl, 79
Tutu, Archbishop Desmond
        Namibia, 80-81
U
Udall, Stewart L.
        Kenya Independence, 59
Uganda, Entebbe
        Nixon Tour, 47-48
United Nations,
        Emperor Haile Selassie at
        UN, 96-97
        Independent Nations, 98-99
United Nations Educational,
        Scientific and Cultural
                Org., (UNESCO), 62
United Negro College Fund, 103
United States
        National Guard, 32
        Navy, 103
        Olympic Committee, 160
V
Van der Zee, James, 155
Vaughn, Sarah, 154
Voting Rights Act, 1965, 33
W
Wagner, Robert F., Mayor

New York City, 97
Walker, Leroy T., President,
        Olympic Committee, U.S., 160
Wallace, Kay, 160
Washington, Denzel, 148
Ward Singers (Clara),18
Waters, Maxine, Rep., (D-Calif.), 86
Watts, Andre, 147
Weaver, Dr. Robert C., 91
West Virginia
        Sleet assignment, 12
Wharton, Clifton R., Jr., 104
White, Cathy, 111
White, Charles, 156
White, Josh, 23
Wilks, John, 117, 123
Wilkins, J. Ernest, Sr.
        Ass't Sec. of Labor, U.S., 89
Wilkins, Roy,
        NAACP, 21-22, 149
Williams, Franklyn H., 91
Williams, Joe, 115
Williams, Mrs. Gertrude
        Johnson, 112, 116
Williams, John T., Dr., 7
Williamson, Tony, 72
Wilson, G. Marshall
        staff photographer and
        colleague, 166
Wilson, Margaret Bush, 114
Wilson, Nancy, 38
Wonder, Stevie, 152
Wood, Thomas, A.
        Young Mission to Africa,

76-79
Woodland, DeVon R.,
        Young Mission to Africa, 79
Woodley, Madeline, 72
Woods, Cerri, 72
Woods, Howard, 113
Wossen, Asfa, Prince (Ethiopia)
        Liberian Independence, 60
Wright, Marian (Edelman), 34-35
        Freedom Summer Cases, 34
Wright, Dr. Stephen
        Liberian Inaugural, 60

Y
Young, Rev. Andrew
        Ambassador, UN, 76-79
        Atlanta, Mayor, 160
        Congress, U.S., 76-79
        Poor Peoples Campaign, 40
        Selma to Montgomery
                March, 33
        Southern Christian
                Leadership Council, 32
Young, Jack, Atty.
        Freedom Summer Cases, 34
Young, Whitney,
        National Urban League, 21-
22, 40
        Death, 103

Z
Zambia, 80
Zie Donis, Arvids Jr., 66